A DIRECTORY OF ADAPTIVE TECHNOLOGIES

TO AID LIBRARY PATRONS AND STAFF WITH DISABILITIES

Dennis A. Norlin

Cay Gasque

Christopher Lewis

Ruth O'Donnell

Lawrence Webster

LITA Monographs 5

Library and Information Technology Association
a division of the
American Library Association
Chicago and London 1994

LITA Monograph Series

No. 1 Library and Information Technology Standards
   Edited by Michael Gorman

No. 2 Access to Information: Materials, Technologies,
   and Services for Print-Impaired Readers
   By Tom McNulty and Dawn M. Suvino

No. 3 Internet Connections: A Librarian's Guide to
   Dial-up Access and Use
   *By Mary E. Engle, Marilyn Lutz, William W. Jones, Jr.,
   and Genevieve Engel*

No. 4 Telecommunications, Networking and
   Internet Glossary
   By George S. Machovec

The paper used in this publication meets the minimum
requirements of American National Standard for Information
Sciences—Permanence of Paper for Printed Library Materials,
ANSI Z39. 48-1984. ∞

Printed on 50-pound acid-free Finch Opaque and bound in 10-point
C1S cover stock by IPC, St. Joseph, Michigan

Library of Congress Cataloging-in-Publication Data
A directory of adaptive technologies to aid library patrons
   and staff with disabilities / by Dennis A. Norlin . . . [et al.].
      p.   cm.
   Includes index.
   ISBN 0-8389-7754-5
   1. Library fittings and supplies—United States—Catalogs.
   2. Libraries and the handicapped—United States.   3. Self-
help devices for the disabled—United States—Catalogs.
   I. Norlin, Dennis A.
   Z684.D57   1994
   020'.29'473—dc20   94-36089

Printed in the United States of America.

98 97 96 95 94   5 4 3 2 1

CONTENTS

INTRODUCTION

In the four years since the Americans with Disabilities Act (ADA) was passed, librarians find themselves confronted with a dizzying amount of information, advice, and warnings about how they should respond to this sweeping new legislation. The purpose of *A Directory of Adaptive Technologies to Aid Library Patrons and Staff with Disabilities* is to provide a one-stop resource on adaptive technology for librarians and library administrators that will: (1) summarize disability-related legislation that affects libraries and librarians; (2) provide guidance for library administrators planning to upgrade the work environment for employees (and future employees) with disabilities to comply with current disability legislation; (3) serve as a reference tool to aid in the identification and selection of assistive devices and technology needed to improve patron access to library services and programs; (4) offer information about organizations that provide support services for people with adaptive technology needs; and (5) identify sources of funding for securing adaptive equipment and technology.

The authors of the *Directory* possess experience in a variety of libraries and with a variety of disabilities and technology. They are all active members of the Adaptive Technologies Interest Group of LITA (Library and Information Technology Association), a division of ALA (American Library Association), and two are former leaders of the Decade of the Disabled Committee of ASCLA (Association of Specialized and Cooperative Library Agencies), another division of ALA.

The impetus for the book came from the Decade of the Disabled Committee's last program: "The Disabled Consumer" (June 30, 1991, at the American Library Association 1991 Annual Conference, Atlanta, Georgia). "The Disabled Consumer" included a preview of the film *People First: Serving and Employing People with Disabilities* (a videotape that highlights three successful library programs that provide services to and employ persons with varying disabilities), a panel of individuals with disabilities who discussed library services to and employment of persons with disabilities from their perspectives as professionals involved with disabilities, and a vendor fair that offered manufacturers and distributors the opportunity to exhibit and demonstrate products to make libraries more accessible and useful to patrons and employees with disabilities.

The expiration of the Decade of the Disabled Committee following the 1991 ALA Annual Meeting, and the ALA decision to abolish the Video and Special Projects office at the same time, meant that librarians who were seeking assistance in responding to the Americans with Disabilities Act (ADA) would have no central source to contact at ALA and no additional audiovisual materials to employ.

The authors view the publication of this *Directory* as an attempt to meet librarians' need for a central reference source that can assist them in obtaining information about effective, affordable, and appropriate technology for persons with disabilities.

The *Directory* differs from other publications of this sort in three major ways:

A. It focuses on equipment and technology that will be of direct use to libraries;

B. It is designed to provide assistance for all kinds of disabilities, not just visual, hearing, and physical impairment;

C. It is designed for ease of use and includes a variety of indexes and cross-references that provide maximum access to the information.

A

Libraries share a number of characteristics with other public institutions: physical facilities, rest room requirements, potential architectural barriers, security and safety concerns, etc. Libraries that have added additions or renovated their physical facilities will, like any other public institution, have to take into account the ADA requirements for physical facilities and access. There are a number of significant resources that will help them make appropriate decisions.

Libraries, of course, also have purposes and are involved in processes that distinguish them from other public institutions. Librarians select, provide access to, and loan materials to patrons; libraries acquire, organize, and retrieve information sources that match information needs of the community; they fill a unique educational role in the community, as resources that adjust themselves to the information needs of their users.

A Directory of Adaptive Technologies to Aid Library Patrons and Staff with Disabilities focuses upon the equipment and technology that is used by library patrons and employees with disabilities and technology that is used primarily to recover, sort and organize, display, and communicate information to users and employees.

B

When the ADA was passed in 1990, 43 million Americans were identified as persons with disabilities. For many librarians, however, like the general population, "disability" usually refers to someone with a visual, hearing, or physical impairment. Consequently, most libraries concentrate their efforts to respond to ADA on these three types of disabilities. This *Directory* attempts to include all kinds of disabilities, including mental retardation, chronic illness, terminal illness, and mental illness.

While it is true that the majority of technological innovations are devoted to the three primary categories of disability, it is also true that some kinds of equipment are useful to people with a variety of disabilities. A computer with a voice synthesizer, for example, may be as valuable for someone with a severe learning disability or mental retardation as it is for someone with a hearing impairment.

C

In the best of all possible worlds, all libraries would be able to afford to buy all the latest adaptive equipment available to serve the needs of their employees and patrons with disabilities. In the real world of budget constraints and cutbacks, however, libraries and their patrons and employees often have to make do with much less than the latest and best technology.

The authors of this *Directory* have tried to make this work usable and practical by providing multiple indexes and cross-references that enable the user to search by cost, type of disability, type of equipment, and vendor. We want this *Directory* to be used, and we have made every effort to make it as easy to use as a restaurant guide.

Conclusion

These considerations have guided the material we have chosen to include in *A Directory of Adaptive Technologies to Aid Library Patrons and Staff with Disabilities*:

1. Is it something that is of direct use to library employees and patrons?

2. Is it useful to persons with a variety of disabilities?

3. Is it easy to locate, relatively inexpensive, reliable?

It is our hope that the information included in this *Directory* will be useful for all types of libraries as they seek to respond to the challenges and opportunities presented by the ADA.

The best way to use this *Directory* is to evaluate your needs, identify the kinds of products that may fill those needs, then contact the vendor to request literature and further discuss your needs, and finally, after reading the literature and perhaps using some of the devices, make your selections.

DENNIS A. NORLIN

CHAPTER **1**

The Law:
Letter and Spirit

Dennis A. Norlin

Although the Americans with Disabilities Act (ADA) (Public Law 101:336) has been the most visible and influential disability legislation of recent times, its passage was made possible by a number of equally significant bills that preceded it during the past two decades. Libraries and librarians seeking to comply with ADA's requirements need to be conversant with at least some of these bills.[1]

In its intent and scope, ADA most closely resembles the Civil Rights Act of 1964. Unlike the 1964 bill's prohibitive nature (proscribing discrimination based upon various categories), however, ADA requires employers' compliance in removing barriers that impede access to employment or services for persons with disabilities.[2] There are four major bills (with amendments) that constitute the legislative background of ADA that are of significance to libraries:[3]

1. The 1973 Rehabilitation Act (Public Law 93:112)

2. The 1975 Developmental Disabilities Assistance and Bill of Rights Act (Public Law 94:103)

---

1. Despite the negative tone of its title, readers are advised to take note of a new book that gives an excellent overview of ADA legislation and its implications for libraries: *How Libraries Must Comply with the Americans with Disabilities Act (ADA)*, edited by Donald D. Foos and Nancy C. Pack (Phoenix: Oryx Press, 1992).

2. *Americans with Disabilities Handbook* (Washington, D.C.: Equal Employment Opportunity Commission and the U.S. Department of Justice, 1991), pp. 1-3.

3. An essential reading list for an overview of this legislation would include the following:

3. The 1975 Education of All Handicapped Children Act (Public Law 94:142) and

4. The 1988 Technology-Related Assistance for Individuals with Disabilities Act (Public Law 100:407).

The first three acts have been amended a number of times, some of the amendments being substantial revisions and others simply renewing the government's commitment, appropriating funds, or revising language.

1. The 1973 Rehabilitation Act (Public Law 93:112)

This landmark legislation was introduced "to replace the Vocational Rehabilitation Act. . . ., with special emphasis on services to those with the most severe handicaps, to expand special Federal responsibilities and research and training programs with respect to the handicapped individuals" and to entrust the Secretary of the (then) Health, Education and Welfare Department (HEW) with responsibility for coordinating all programs for persons with disabilities.[4]

The 1973 Act was very broad in scope, but also included some very specific provisions. Section 305, for example, established a National Center for Deaf-Blind Youths and Adults; Section 502 established the Architectural and Transportation Barriers Compliance Board. The federal government's support for adaptive equipment and technology was assured in Section 202: Research, when the bill provided for the establishment of Rehabilitation Engineering Research Centers.[5]

Most controversial of all, however, was Section 504: Nondiscrimination under Federal Grants. Challenges to Section 504 resulted in seventeen Supreme Court decisions, and a wide range of agency regulations specifying the implications of the

---

Americans with Disabilities Act Handbook, published by the Equal Employment Opportunity Commission and the U.S. Department of Justice (Washington, D.C.: United States Government Printing Office, 1991).

K. L. Reed, "History of Federal Legislation for Persons with Disabilities," *American Journal of Occupational Therapy* 46:5 (May, 1992), pp. 397–408.

Lowell P. Weicker, Jr., "Historical Background of the Americans with Disabilities Act," *Temple Law Review* 64 (1991), pp. 387–392.

4. *United States Statutes at Large,* vol. 87 (Washington, D.C.: United States Government Printing Office, 1974), p. 355.

5. *Ibid.,* pp. 375–376.

section.[6] Enforcement of ADA requirements is patterned after Section 504 and is vested with the Equal Employment Opportunity Commission (EEOC).

There have been many amendments to P.L. 93:112 in the past twenty years, but two have special significance in the area of technology for persons with disabilities.

A. Public Law 95:602. The 1978 Rehabilitation Comprehensive Services and Developmental Disabilities Act

This bill established a community service employment program and provided comprehensive services for independent living for persons with disabilities. It also established Developmental Disabilities Councils on functional impairments and identified priority areas.

Section 104 mandated "the use of existing telecommunications systems (including telephone, television, satellite, radio, and other similar systems) which have the potential for substantially improving service delivery methods and the development of appropriate programming to meet the particular needs of handicapped individuals" and added "the use of services providing recorded material for the blind and captioned films or video cassettes for the deaf."[7]

Section 202 established a National Institute of Handicapped Research within HEW that had the task of collecting, coordinating, and disseminating information about research in rehabilitation. Section 203 established in the federal government an Interagency Committee on Handicapped Research charged with "identifying, assessing, and coordinating all Federal programs, activities and projects. . . . related to the rehabilitation of handicapped individuals."[8]

Section 204 established Rehabilitation Research and Training Centers to be operated in collaboration with institutions of higher education, while Section 314 expanded "the quality and scope of reading services available to blind persons" including braille, sound recordings, and equipment providing access to printed materials by mechanical or electronic means.[9]

---

6. *Ibid.,* p. 394. Very brief, Section 504 nonetheless proved to be very controversial:

> No otherwise qualified handicapped individual in the United States, as defined in section 7 (6), shall, solely by reason of his handicap, be excluded from the participation in, be denied the benefits of, or be subjected to discrimination under any program or activity receiving Federal financial assistance.

7. *United States Statutes at Large,* vol. 92, Part 3 (Washington, D.C.: United States Government Printing Office, 1980), p. 2960.

8. *Ibid.,* pp. 2963–2965.

9. *Ibid.,* pp. 2966–2967, 2975.

Section 401 established the National Council on the Handicapped charged, among other things, with reviewing the operation of the National Institute of Handicapped Research.[10]

B. Public Law 99:506. Rehabilitation Act Amendments of 1986

This bill provided for special demonstration programs that would meet the needs of isolated populations of persons with disabilities, including recreational programs, and also defined the mission and purpose of the National Council on the Handicapped.

It also revised Section 508 that established guidelines on electronic equipment accessibility: "The Secretary, through the National Institute on Disability and Rehabilitation Research and the Administrator of General Services, in consultation with the electronics industry, shall develop and establish guidelines for electronic equipment accessibility designed to insure that handicapped individuals may use electronic office equipment with or without special peripherals."[11]

2. The 1975 Developmental Disabilities Assistance and Bill of Rights Act (Public Law 94:103)

The second major precursor of the ADA was a 1975 bill that extended the government's full range of support services to the developmentally disabled. The bill defined developmental disability as:

. . . a severe, chronic disability of a person which—

(A) is attributable to a mental or physical impairment or combination of mental and physical impairments;

(B) is manifested before the person attains the age twenty-two;

(C) is likely to continue indefinitely;

(D) results in substantial functional limitations in three or more of the following areas of major life activity: (i) self-care, (ii) receptive and expressive language, (iii) learning, (iv) mobility, (v) self-direction, (vi) capacity for independent living, and (vii) economic self-sufficiency; and

---

10. *Ibid.*, pp. 2977–2983.

11. *United States Statutes at Large,* vol. 100, Part 2 (Washington, D.C.: United States Government Printing Office, 1989), pp. 1830–1831.

(E) reflects the person's need for a combination and sequence of special, interdisciplinary, or generic care, treatment, or other services which are of lifelong or extended duration and are individually planned and coordinated.[12]

In addition to mandating services for persons with developmental disabilities, this bill established university-affiliated facilities and provided demonstration and training grants to support their efforts to provide appropriate training and habilitation for persons with developmental disabilities.

Several amendments have been added to this bill in the past eighteen years; two have special importance for libraries: (1) the 1984 Amendments, P.L. 98:527 Independent Living Facilities, and (2) the 1987 Amendments, P.L. 100:146 Training and Early Intervention. The first bill was intended to enable persons with developmental disabilities to "achieve their maximum potential through increased independence, productivity, and integration into the community" and to ensure their legal and human rights.[13] The 1986 amendments mandated suitable employment and habilitation plans for developmentally disabled persons.

Public Law 100:146 also amended the 1975 Developmental Disabilities Assistance and Bill of Rights Act. It highlighted the need to "enable such persons to achieve their maximum potential through increased independence, productivity, and integration into the community," and the importance of enhancing the role of the family in supporting the individual and of ensuring that disabled persons' rights were safeguarded and protected.[14]

3. The 1975 Education of All Handicapped Children Act (Public Law 94:142)

Also passed in 1975, Public Law 94:142 had a major impact on all educational institutions in the United States. Mandating the education of persons with disabilities in the least restrictive environment, P.L. 94–142 introduced the whole system of planning each affected person's education through the use of Individual Educational Profiles (IEPs). Section 653 of the bill encouraged educational and other nonprofit agencies "for the establishment and operation of centers on educational

---

12. *United States Statutes at Large,* vol. 89 (Washington, D.C.: United States Government Printing Office, 1977), p. 497.

13. *United States Statutes at Large,* vol. 98, Part 3 (Washington, D.C.: United States Government Printing Office, 1986), p. 2663.

14. *United States Statutes at Large,* vol. 101, Part 1 (Washington, D.C.: United States Government Printing Office, 1989), p. 841.

media and materials for the handicapped, which together will provide a comprehensive program of activities to facilitate the use of new educational technology in education programs for handicapped persons, including designing, developing, and adapting instructional materials. . . ."[15]

One amendment to P.L. 94:142 has had significance for the development and use of technology by persons with disabilities. Public Law 99:457 (Education of the Handicapped Amendments of 1986) expands the impact of P.L. 99:142 by mandating an early intervention program to provide disability services for infants and toddlers with disabilities. Clearly the intent of P.L. 99:457 was to provide a wide variety of services that would meet all of the person's developmental needs—physical development, cognitive development, language and speech development, psychosocial development, and self-help skills. By focusing upon the family's role (through the use of an Individualized Family Service Plan—IFSP), this bill involved the family as equal partners with schools and social service agencies in planning for their child's future. The implementation of P.L. 99:457 is more broadly interpreted than the original bill, and can include a variety of services and programs needed by the family of the affected child.[16]

Although few libraries have become involved in the process of implementing this bill, families certainly have an enormous need for information about available resources that could best be met by libraries serving as "community information centers . . . (that) can link parents and service providers to best meet the specialized needs of the families of children with disabilities." Public libraries also qualify, under this bill, to receive funding to distribute captioned films and other educational media and equipment.[17]

4. The 1988 Technology-Related Assistance for Individuals with Disabilities Act (Public Law 100:407)

This 1988 law was designed to recognize and utilize the new advances in technology that could be of assistance to persons with disabilities in their employment and education. The bill defined the benefits of assistive technology to persons with disabilities:

15. *United States Statutes at Large,* vol. 89 (Washington, D.C.: United States Government Printing Office, 1977), p. 795.

16. *United States Statutes at Large,* vol. 100, Part 2 (Washington, D.C.: United States Government Printing Office, 1989), pp. 1145–1177.

17. Christopher Lewis, "Public Law 99–457: The Librarian's Perspective," *Library Access: Services for People with Disabilities* 1:2 (April, 1991), pp. 1–3.

The provision of assistive technology devices and assistive technology services enables some individuals with disabilities to—

(A)   have greater control over their own lives;

(B)   participate in and contribute more fully to activities in their homes, school, and work environments, and in their communities;

(C)   interact to a greater extent with non-disabled individuals; and

(D)   otherwise benefit from opportunities that are taken for granted by individuals who do not have disabilities.[18]

The bill encourages states to develop an increased awareness of the needs of individuals with disabilities for assistive technology devices and service and to increase the availability of funding for those devices and services.

Two important definitions were established in this act: *assistive technology device* and *assistive technology service.* An assistive technology device is defined as "any item, piece of equipment, or product system, whether acquired commercially off the shelf, modified, or customized, that is used to increase, maintain, or improve functional capabilities of individuals with disabilities."[19]

Assistive technology service, on the other hand, was more fully described:

(A)   the evaluation of the needs of an individual with a disability, including a functional evaluation of the individual in the individual's customary environment;

(B)   purchasing, leasing, or otherwise providing for the acquisition of assistive technology devices by individuals with disabilities;

(C)   selecting, designing, fitting, customizing, adapting, applying, maintaining, repairing, or replacing of assistive technology devices;

(D)   coordinating and using other therapies, interventions or services with assistive technology devices, such as those associated with existing education and rehabilitation plans and programs;

(E)   training or technical assistance for an individual with disabilities, or, where appropriate, the family of an individual with disabilities; and

(F)   training or technical assistance for professionals (including individuals providing education and rehabilitation services), employers, or

18. *United States Statutes at Large,* vol. 102, Part 2 (Washington, D.C.: United States Government Printing Office, 1990), p. 1045.

19. *Ibid.,* p. 1046

other individuals who provide services to, employ, or are otherwise substantially involved in the major life functions of individuals with disabilities.[20]

The 1988 bill also sought to study the development of a national information and program referral network that would "assist States to develop and implement consumer-responsive statewide programs of technology-related assistance."[21]

For nearly twenty years prior to the passage of the Americans with Disabilities Act, then, the federal government had been moving in the direction of stronger and more extensive support for persons with disabilities and was already promoting the utilization of assistive technology devices and services to enable persons with disabilities to participate more fully in all aspects of society. Despite these notable efforts of the federal government, however, many people, both disabled and non-disabled, remained unaware of these dramatic changes.

Libraries, like many other institutions, often failed to take advantage of the opportunity to participate in this movement to support persons with disabilities. And, like much of the rest of the population, many libraries were taken by surprise when the Americans with Disabilities Act passed in 1990.

Public Law 101-336
The Americans with Disabilities Act of 1990

There have been thousands of articles written, workshops conducted, and symposiums held about this landmark bill and its implications for our society, and yet a great deal of the intense discussion and concern about the bill has failed to capture the spirit and concern of this legislation. The tone of the bill is set in its title: *To establish a clear and comprehensive prohibition of discrimination on the basis of disability.*[22] Everything in the bill is designed to support the goal stated in the title, and librarians are well-advised to read the actual bill in its entirety before approaching the massive secondary literature. ADA consists of 5 titles: Employment, Public Services, Public Accommodations and Services Operated by Private Entities, Telecommunications, and Miscellaneous.[23]

---

20. *Ibid.*, p. 1047.

21. *Ibid.*, p. 1060.

22. *Americans with Disabilities Act Handbook* (Washington, D.C.: United States Government Printing Office, 1991), Appendix A, p. 1.

23. *Ibid.*

Title I. Employment

Title I prohibits discrimination at any point in hiring, training, or establishing conditions of employment, and in addition it requires employers to make *reasonable accommodations* to provide suitable employment conditions for persons with disabilities unless making those accommodations would constitute an *undue hardship* for the institution.

In the case of hiring this title intends to eliminate tests that would unfairly screen out or tend to screen out applicants with disabilities. Any tests of employment, therefore, must accurately reflect the applicant's skills and abilities. Any job standards and criteria that are conditions of employment must be job-related and can exclude someone with a disability only if they cannot be adapted through *reasonable accommodation.*

Unfortunately, many institutions have spent more energy, time, and effort trying to establish incontestable conditions of employment than they have exploring ways to provide reasonable accommodation for persons with disabilities. For example, a condition of employment might be "must be able to lift boxes weighing 50 pounds" even though the person in the position rarely, if ever, has to perform this task. Using a criteria like this might enable an institution to exclude many people with disabilities, but misses the very spirit of ADA!

This *Directory* is designed to support libraries that intend to support more than the letter of the law in response to ADA by providing information about inexpensive and helpful adaptive equipment and technology that will enable their employees, whatever their physical or mental limitations, to perform the responsibilities assigned them.

Title II. Public Services

The second title of ADA mandates nondiscrimination by any business, agency, or institution in its treatment of the general public: no qualified individual with disabilities shall be excluded from *participation in* or *denied the benefits* of services, programs, or activities of a public entity.[24]

Although the majority of Title II is devoted to public transportation regulations, section A (Prohibition against Discrimination and Other Generally Applicable Provisions) sets the tone for public services that are more fully described in Title III.

---

24. *Ibid.*, Section 202, p. 11.

Title III. Public Accommodations and Services Operated by Private Entities

Title III delineates public accommodations by category and includes libraries in section H: *a museum, library, gallery, or other place of public display or collection.*[25] Title III more fully explains the responsibilities of public accommodations in providing services to persons with disabilities. Everyone is entitled to "full and equal enjoyment of the goods, services, facilities, privileges, advantages, or accommodations of any place of public accommodation."[26]

Public accommodations are required to provide benefits and services that are equal and integrated. Providing separate services for persons with disabilities is forbidden "unless such action is necessary to provide the individual or class of individuals with a good, service, facility, privilege, advantage, or accommodation, or other opportunity that is as effective as that provided to others."[27]

Title III requires public accommodations, including libraries, to (i) refrain from using any eligibility criteria that tend to screen out any individuals with disabilities, (ii) make reasonable accommodations in policies, practices, and procedures necessary to afford goods, services, facilities, privileges, advantages, or accommodations to individuals with disabilities, (iii) take steps to ensure that individuals with disabilities are not "excluded, denied services, segregated or otherwise treated differently" than other individuals "because of the absence of auxiliary aids and services," and, (iv) remove architectural and communication barriers that are structural in nature.[28]

Each of these requirements has an "escape clause" in Title III. The requirement to refrain from imposing eligibility criteria, for example, is waived if it "can be shown to be necessary for the provision of the goods, services, facilities, privileges, advantages, or accommodations being offered."[29] But the thrust of each requirement is positive—to make accommodation, to find alternatives, to provide adaptive equipment and techniques so that all potential patrons will have full use of the library's resources and services.

---

25. *Ibid*, Section 301, p. 26.
26. *Ibid.,* Section 302, p. 27.
27. *Ibid.,* Section 302 A (iii), p. 28.
28. *Ibid.,* Section 302 (2), Specific prohibitions, pp. 28–29.
29. *Ibid.,* p. 28.

Title IV. Telecommunications

Title IV of ADA applies primarily to common carriers engaged in interstate communication by wire or radio to mandate services that facilitate two-way communication that includes individuals with speech or hearing impairments and closed captioning of public service announcements.[30]

Title V. Miscellaneous

Title V covers a variety of areas including construction requirements, prohibition of retaliation or coercion against those who exercise their rights to complain or protest conditions of employment or service mandated in the act, regulation of the architectural and transportation barriers compliance board, development of a plan to provide technical assistance to organizations covered under ADA, and several other areas, including some exclusions from the definition "individual with disability." Transvestites (yes, they *are* singled out!) and drug users are *not* considered to be individuals with disabilities.[31]

Libraries share with all other "public accommodations" the responsibility to respond to the ADA to the best of their ability. Like many other institutions in our litigious society, however, libraries may tend to adopt a defensive posture in response to ADA, seeking to define limits to their responsibilities. The authors of this *Directory* believe that there are strong reasons for libraries to adopt a proactive, creative effort to fulfill not only the requirements but also the spirit of ADA.

ADA does not stand alone; America has a long history of legislative attempts to more fully include people with disabilities in the mainstream of American culture and society. As fundamental democratic institutions of our society, America's libraries, public, academic, and special, should be leaders in demonstrating creative and thoughtful ways to encourage that inclusion. This *Directory* should help libraries, even libraries with very limited budgets and resources, to take steps in the direction of full inclusion of persons with disabilities on their staff and as their patrons.

---

30. *Ibid.,* Section 401, pp. 37, 40.
31. *Ibid.,* pp. 40–48.

CHAPTER 2

The State of the Art in Assistive Technology

Product descriptions of assistive technology devices
useful in all libraries to aid patrons and employees

Christopher Lewis

The Americans with Disabilities Act is a mandate for businesses and institutions to provide people with disabilities with equal access to all services and activities available to the public and to provide reasonable accommodations to qualified job applicants to enable them to perform duties required in a position. Assistive devices are an important factor in the provision of services to many individuals with disabilities; in fact, the law requires that they be provided when their cost will not cause an undue burden on the organization. Because the law is new and the term *assistive technology* is in its infancy, it can be difficult to locate the variety of specialized devices helpful in aiding employees and patrons.

This chapter describes some of the latest devices available that would be useful in a library environment. An effort has been made to include as many devices as possible, so the inclusion or exclusion of a particular device does not reflect an evaluative decision on the author's part.

Often a particular device will have unique features that make it difficult to compare it fairly to another device from the same general category. In addition, the sheer number of devices included made it virtually impossible to "test drive" each one, so our objective is to be informative rather than evaluative. Prices are included, but they should only be used as general guidelines. Current price information is available from the vendor or producer listed in chapter 3.

The flexibility of personal computers has enabled many inventors and product designers to develop add-on devices to further personalize the computer for an individual's needs. These products have enabled individuals with disabilities to perform tasks with the computer that they previously were incapable of performing. Examples include speech synthesizers, alternative keyboards and memory resident software for screen enlargement or keystroke control.

Because many of the products listed depend upon computers, system compatibility should be of paramount concern to the prospective buyer. Some products, for example, may require an operating system at a level higher than the buyer owns or may have hardware requirements that aren't always apparent. Where possible the original manufacturer's name is included but several devices (and the literature about them) are available only through distributors.

There is much overlap among distributors in regard to certain products. For instance, Ultratec TDDs can be bought directly from the company or can be purchased from several different distributors. Often buying directly from the manufacturer will be less expensive but also less convenient in regard to maintenance needs. It is advisable to make servicing convenience a high priority when considering purchase of any high-use mechanical or electronic device. It is left to the reader to determine the best source for a given product.

Several of the product categories included in this book may appear to be beyond the requirements of what the Americans with Disabilities Act mandates for patrons. An example would be voice recognition software that would require a fair amount of adjusting to fit an individual's speech patterns. This kind of software is intended to be used by a single user and wouldn't be usable by other individuals. It is included here because it may be needed for a library employee to perform his or her job better. The needs of an employee must be addressed a little differently than those of a patron.

This chapter is arranged in four loosely defined sections: hearing and speech impairments, mobility impairments, low vision, and blindness. These categories are broad enough to include devices of use to individuals with learning disabilities, developmental disabilities, chronic diseases, spinal and traumatic brain injuries, and other disabilities.

The kinds of products that will be of particular interest to individuals with hearing and speech impairments include amplification devices, Telecommunication Devices for the Deaf (TDDs), signalling devices, and closed caption decoders.

The term *mobility impairments* includes disabilities restricting the use of body movement. For individuals with erratic movement or limited use of arms or hands, there are numerous computer modifications available including keyguards, override auto-repeat, input redundancy (this program allows use of keyboard or voice input in addition to a standard mouse input), single finger programs, keylatches for temporary locking, keyboard redefinition (to redistribute typing load more evenly between fingers on one hand), and miniature keyboards. Alternative input methods—switches, switch interfaces, scanning, morse code, direct selection—using eyegaze, head pointer, or light beam, and voice recognition are important alternatives for persons with mobility impairments.

The term *visual disabilities* includes individuals with impaired sight as well as individuals with complete blindness. Examples of products include magnification software, magnification lenses, large key markings, large character and more readable fonts for printers, braillers, braille printers, braille keyboard markings, speech synthesizers, optical readers, word processors with synthesized speech output, talking calculators, and a variety of alternatives to printed format.

The term *learning disabilities* in this chapter encompasses attention deficit disorder, autism, dyslexia, mental retardation, and other disabilities that affect learning. The kinds of devices that will be of interest to patrons with learning disabilities include computer software that provides visual cues through graphics and animation, auditory cues through voice, music, and sound prompts, and tactile cues through keyboard or touchscreen.

Many types of devices do not fall conveniently into a single category so we have put them into the category representing the group of users likely to use them most and then included notations of any advantages they might provide to other users. An example is voice synthesizing software that translates screen text to electronic speech. This software would be useful for individuals with impaired vision and learning disabilities but would probably be of most use to the blind individual, so these products are included under that heading. Products made for people with vision impairments will often be useful to individuals with learning disabilities. Large membrane keyboards made primarily for people with physical disabilities will also be helpful to people with learning disabilities. People with speech impairments can benefit from using TDDs although they are used primarily by individuals with hearing loss.

Investing in adaptive equipment for individuals with disabilities will also benefit other patrons in addition to those without recognized disabilities. Wider aisles and lower shelves usually result in better lighting conditions and easier access for everyone. Book holders or adjustable seating also make an environment more comfortable for all patrons, as do various magnifying devices.

Assistive computer technology can be divided into two general conceptual categories: input devices and output devices.

1. Input devices include the variety of products that enable users to input and manipulate information in a computer. The most common input devices are the keyboard and the mouse. The mouse has proven to be popular among many users including those with limited motor abilities. The standard keyboard however can be difficult for many users to access. Both keyboard enhancements and keyboard alternatives are available to provide keyboard access to most individuals.

2. Output devices include the products that provide alternatives to the standard computer monitor and printer. Examples include braille printers, screen magnifiers, and voice synthesizers.

There are many "mainstream" products that are particularly useful to individuals with disabilities and it is suggested that the following features be considered when making equipment selections:

For hearing impairments

Try to ensure that any software selections incorporating audible cues have visual redundancy (e.g., the dialing sound of a modem and visual display indicating dialing).

Emergency devices and telephones should have flashing lights in addition to sound signalling.

Electronic mail systems provide a fast, convenient means for everyone to communicate and may be a preferred means of communicating for individuals with hearing or speech impairments.

Fax machines can also be particularly useful to individuals with hearing or speech impairments for much the same reason as an electronic mail system.

All new television/monitors purchased should have the ability to display closed captioning.

For mobility impairments

Adjustable seating and desk/table tops can make the library environment more comfortable for a wide variety of patrons.

For visual impairments

Computers that have the option of changing the colors of the display will benefit color-blind users.

A glare protection screen will make any computer monitor much easier to read for most reading patrons.

Computer printers should have scalable fonts.

A large computer monitor will also be more easily read by individuals with vision impairments.

Categories of Products

1.0 FOR HEARING AND SPEECH

1.1 **Amplification**—devices for electronically amplifying sound for hearing impaired individuals.

    1.1a Telephones

1.2 **Captioning**—devices that produce a textual display of spoken communications.

    1.2a Closed Caption Display Televisions

    1.2b Closed Caption Auxiliary Devices

    1.2c Caption-Producing Software

1.3 **Telecommunication Devices for the Deaf (TDDs)**—TDDs provide telephone access to patrons with hearing impairments, complete hearing loss, or speech impairments.

1.4 **Other Telecommunications Devices**—These devices adapt standard phones for individuals with all types of disabilities.

    1.4a Telephone Headsets

    1.4b Other Telephone Aids

1.5 **In-Person Communication**—devices that amplify voices in face-to-face communication.

1.6 **Signaling Devices**— visual equivalents of signaling devices that normally use audible signals, such as fire alarms, smoke detectors, and telephones.

1.7 **Visual Redundancy for Computers**—visual signals that reinforce any audio signals (e.g., beeps) that many types of computer software incorporate in their operation.

1.8 **Speech Training Technology**—programs and devices that aid in speech training and therapy.

2.0 FOR MOBILITY

2.1 **Keyboard Modifications**—accessories that can modify a keyboard so it can be more efficiently used by individuals with unsteady hand movement.

    2.1a Keyguards and Keylocks—protect against unintentionally pressing unneeded keys.

2.1b Disk Guides—aid in the insertion of floppy disks into floppy drives.

2.2 **Mouth Stick or Head Stick**—pointing devices that can be held in one's mouth or attached to a headband. Useful for pressing keys and buttons.

2.3 **Augmentative Hand Devices**—pointing devices that can be grasped in one's hand. Useful for accessing keyboards, telephones, etc.

2.4 **Page Turners**—enable individuals with limited hand or arm movement to more easily read books, magazines, and other texts.

2.5 **Door Knobs**—door handles are much easier to grasp than door knobs. There are also door handle adapters that fit over door knobs.

2.6 **Alternative Computer Monitors**

2.7 **Alternative Computer Input**—a device that provides an alternative to the standard keyboard and mouse input.

  2.7a Keyboard Enhancement Programs—software programs that enable slower typers to speed up and also adapt keyboards for efficient use with one hand.

  2.7b Keyboard Enhancement Hardware

  2.7c Speech Recognition/Voice Input

  2.7d Alternative Keyboards—non-traditional alphanumeric keyboards designed for individuals who have difficulty typing on a standard keyboard.

  2.7e Larger (or Expanded) Keyboards—typically touch-sensitive membrane surface divided into squares representing keys. Some models have the ability to reprogram the position of the keys.

  2.7f Smaller Keyboards—recommended for users with a limited range of motion in their hands, wrists, or arms.

  2.7g Touch Screens—user inputs information into the computer by touching commands on the screen. Valuable for users who have difficulty accessing a standard keyboard or a mouse.

  2.7h Mouse Entry—alternative to standard computer mouse entry, which moves the cursor around the screen in the same way.

  2.7i Joystick Entry—identical to the kind of joystick used in many video games, this kind of device allows a user to navigate around a keyboard like a mouse.

2.7j Interface Card/Hardware and Software—the components needed to make alternative input devices work with standard computer software.

2.7k On-Screen Keyboards—useful for patrons or employees who are unable to type on a standard keyboard.

2.7l Word Processing Programs—user friendly word processing software designed for users with disabilities.

2.7m Morse Code Software—allows morse code input, from among a variety of switches, to be translated to alphanumeric characters.

2.7n Switches—enable use of a computer without using a keyboard or mouse. Wide variety: sip & puff, head/finger/arm/wrist control.

2.8 **Optimal Positioning**—These devices allow the user to adjust the physical environment to better suit his or her range of motion.

3.0 FOR LOW VISION

3.1 **Large Character Display**—products for increasing the size of alphanumeric characters to be more easily read by individuals with vision impairments or learning disabilities.

3.1a Large Button Telephone

3.1b Large Print Typewriter

3.1c Computer Keyboards—labels and keycaps with larger alphanumeric characters to be put over standard keytops.

3.1d Software—memory resident software that enlarges the text of other software being used.

3.1e Copying Machine with Enlarging—most major copying machine manufacturers have models with enlarging capabilities.

3.1f Magnifying Lenses for Reading Print Materials—standard handheld and desk models.

3.1g Magnifying Lens for Computer Monitor—an external lens that fits on the front of the computer monitor.

3.1h Magnifying Lens for Television Screen

3.1i Closed Circuit TV (CCTV) Systems—Closed circuit television systems are used to electronically magnify printed text, maps, diagrams, objects, etc.

4.0 FOR BLINDNESS

4.1 **Braille Writing and Embossing Equipment**—braille "typewriters."

4.2 **Braille Input Devices**—braille-making keyboards that produce code that is translated into computer text.

4.3 **Keyboards/Keytops**—accessories to help the blind user locate keys on the computer keyboard.

4.4 **Braille Output Devices**—paperless braille displays and braille printer/embossers.

  4.4a Screen Access/Paperless Braille Displays—braille output devices that enable blind users to navigate computer screens. Smooth-tipped pins electronically pop up or retract to create the braille characters of whatever word or line is highlighted on the screen.

4.5 **Braille Translation Software (from print to braille)**—this software converts computer text to braille code for use with paperless braille devices and braille printer/embossers.

4.6 **Braille Printers/Embossers**—instead of printing with ink, braille printer/embossers press braille dots onto the paper. Some models are capable of both ink printing and braille embossing simultaneously.

4.7 **Text-to-Speech Synthesizers**—internal and external voice synthesizers are used to translate computer text into spoken words.

  4.7a Internal Synthesizers—peripheral card that is inserted into the computer and provides voice output. No external devices are required.

  4.7b External Synthesizers/Speakers—usually a self-contained "add-on" component. Some models will require text-to-speech translation software. Typically includes the synthesizer and a connecting cable.

4.8 **Text-to-Speech Software for Synthesizers**—software that converts computer text to speech code to be used with a speech synthesizer.

4.9 **Optical Character Scanner**—device used for sweeping across printed page to transfer alphanumeric characters to computer readable format so they can be speech synthesized, turned into braille, or otherwise electronically manipulated.

4.10 **Optical Character Recognition (OCR) Systems**—systems and devices that can "read" printed text aloud or can translate that information into a computer file so it can be translated into braille.

4.11 **Other Devices and Tools**

Products by Category

(Products Listed Alphabetically by Vendor)

Note: Numbers in brackets [ ] refer to the company description listing in chapter 3.
$ symbols indicate the approximate cost:

$	=	$	0—$	99	
$$	=	$	100—$	250	
$$$	=	$	251—$	499	
$$$$	=	$	500—$	999	
$$$$$	=	$	1,000—$9,999		
$$$$$+	=	$10,000—			

Citation Format

Brand Name (or Generic Name)

Brief Description

Computer Compatibility

Price

Vendor

[ ] Vendor Identification Number in chapter 3

$$$ Cost Symbol

Listings within categories are arranged alphabetically by vendor. Although most products have very brief listings, many products are accompanied by short descriptions to better illustrate the category.

1.0 FOR HEARING AND SPEECH

1.1 **Amplification**—devices for electronically amplifying sound for hearing impaired individuals.

  1.1a Telephones

  Amplified Transmitter Handsets
  Walker Equipment Corp.   [132] $

  Hearing Amplification Handsets. Amplifies volume from 30% to 45%.
  AT&T Accessible Communications Product Center   [17] $

1.2 **Captioning**—devices that produce a textual display of spoken communications.

  1.2a Closed Caption Auxiliary Devices

  Telecaption 4000 Decoder. Reveals text of closed captioned programs on television screen.
  AT&T Accessible Communications Product Center   [17] $$

  1.2b Caption-Producing Software

  CPC-500: The CaptionMaker. IBM-compatible software capable of producing open and closed captioning for existing videotapes.
  Computer Prompting and Captioning Company   [29] $$$$

1.3 **Telecommunication Devices for the Deaf (TDDs)**—TDDs provide telephone access to patrons with hearing impairments or complete hearing loss. They are also valuable devices for individuals with speech impairments. They are necessary for libraries that offer phone-in reference and renewals among their services. The variety of available models include simple stand-alone units, printing models, and internal computer programs that work with modems. They are all easy to use and relatively inexpensive.

  Text Telephone 2830
  AT&T Accessible Communications Product Center   [17] $$$$

  Text Telephone 2710
  AT&T Accessible Communications Product Center   [17] $$$

PV Jr., MP20, and MP20D
AT&T Accessible Communications Product Center   [17] $$$$

Portaview Jr. and Sr., Portaview Plus, Memory Printer, Porta
   Printer IV
KRI Communications, Inc.   [77] $$$

MIC300i Internal Modem TDD and FullTalk. Features include help
   screens, choice of colors, ability to talk with TDDs or comput-
   ers, 2 dialing directories, word-wrap, answering machine with
   remote access, incoming call flash, and scrolling. PC, PS/2.
Microflip, Inc.   [85] $$$

Modem (CM-4) and TDD; Emulator Software for PC
Phone-TTY, Inc.   [97] $$$; $

Supercom, Miniprint II, Superprint Line, Compact, Minicom III
   and IV. Also Large Visual Display for TDD users.
Ultratec, Inc.   [124] $$

Other TDD Manufacturers:

   Eastern Electronics Corporation   [41] $$
   Nationwide Flashing Signal Systems   [93] $$$

1.4   **Other Telecommunications Devices**—These devices adapt standard
phones for individuals with all types of disabilities. Some of the devices listed
here are more appropriate for library employees than for library patrons
owing to the nature of their use. For example, telephone ring signalers and
headsets are suited to individuals who have considerable dependence on the
phone in their day-to-day business.

   1.4a   Telephone Headsets

      Dynamate 1200. Includes earphone, microphone, and seven-foot
         cord with modular jack. Other models also available.
      ACS Technologies, Inc.   [6] $

   1.4b   Other Telephone Aids

      InfoTouch. A communication system for deaf and blind braille
         readers. Messages are typed in six-key braille or QWERTY and
         displayed in five seconds on Romeo Braille printer. Typed

messages are transmitted by telephone through Superprint modem. Presence of caller at other end of line signaled by Vibrating Data Detector.
Enabling Technologies Company   [46] $$$$$

Portable Terminals. Laptop computer with speech synthesis.
HumanWare, Inc.   [64] $$$$$

Speakwriter 2000. Typewriter (Brother CX-90) with speech synthesis.
HumanWare, Inc.   [64] $$$$$

IBM PhoneCommunicator. Permits a PC to be used as a TDD. Features auto-answer, programmable modem, auto dialing of preprogrammed numbers.
IBM Independence Series Information Center   [65] $$$$

Telebraille II. This system includes both a standard TDD unit and a modified TDD with braille input and output for deaf-blind users. It can be used for both telephone conversations and face-to-face conversations.
Telesensory Systems, Inc.   [118] $$$$$

1.5   **In-Person Communication**—devices that amplify voices in face-to-face communication.

SpeakEasy. Small, portable message machine that plays up to 12 messages by using built-in keyboard or external switches. Messages can be customized. Symbols indicate type of message.
Don Johnston, Inc.   [35] $$$

Picture Communication Symbols. 2,500 symbols/drawings that can be use as individual communication aids.
Don Johnston, Inc.   [35] $

IntroTalker. Simple, lightweight communication device allows up to 64 messages; up to two minutes of extended speech.
Prentke Romich Company   [102] $$$$

Opticommunicator. Allows nonverbal paralyzed persons to communicate with their eyes by focusing upon the picture, word, or letter needed.
Cestwood Company   [32] $

23

Touch Talker, Light Talker. Intermediate DECtalk speech communication devices with flexible configuration and the ability to control telephone, lights, television, etc.
Prentke Romich Company   [102] $$$$$

Liberator. A complete communication tool for non-speaking people, including speech synthesis, text editing, with access by touch, pointer, switch, or infrared pointing system.
Prentke Romich Company   [102] $$$$$

1.6   **Signaling Devices**—visual equivalents of signaling devices that normally use audible signals, such as fire alarms, smoke detectors, and telephones.

Tone Ringer. Emits a telephone ring in a special frequency range (750 to 1500 Hz) that can be heard by many people with hearing impairments.
AT&T Accessible Communications Product Center   [17] $

Signalman. Visually signals incoming calls.
AT&T Accessible Communications Product Center   [17] $

Gentex Smoke Detector with Visual Signaling Strobe. Open area or wall mount or portable model.
Demco, Inc.   [33] $$

Sonic Alert. Telephone ring signaler.
Harris Communications   [57] $

Telephone Aids
Nationwide Flashing Signal Systems   [93] $

End-O-Line-Lite. Flashing light for IBM Selectric of SCM 2500 typewriters, replaces bell at end of line.
Typewriting Institute for the Handicapped   [123] $$

1.7   **Visual Redundancy for Computers**—visual signals that reinforce any audio signals (e.g., beeps) that many types of computer software incorporate in their operation.

SeeBEEP. Visual beep facility. One can either flash the entire screen or just flash the word "Beep" at the cursor location for up to 2 seconds. Software and manual. PC, PS/2.
Microsystems Software Inc.   [87] $

1.8 **Speech Training Technology**—programs and devices that aid in speech training and therapy.

> Articulation/Language Object Kit. 73 familiar objects stored in 4 boxes by position of speech sounds: initial, medial, final consonants, and blends.
> Crestwood Company   [32] $$

> Auditory Training Unit. Two-headphone set with tape recorder that allows clinician to work directly with client in simultaneous or recorded feedback.
> Crestwood Company   [32] $$

> SpeechViewer II. A full-function speech modification/therapy program for PC.
> IBM Independence Series Information Center   [65] $$$$$

2.0 FOR MOBILITY

2.1 **Keyboard Modifications**—keyboard accessories that can modify a keyboard so it can be more efficiently used by individuals with unsteady hand movement.

> 2.1a Keyguards and Keylocks—protect against unintentionally pressing unneeded keys.
>
> Keylock Light Indicators. PC.
> ARTS Computer Products, Inc.   [16] $
>
> Keyguards. PC, Apple II, Commodore 64, VIC 20.
> Don Johnston, Inc.   [35] $
>
> Stick-on Keylocks, Spring-loaded Keylocks. Fit most computer keyboards.
> Extensions for Independence   [50] $
>
> KeyStopper Kit; FlexShield Keyboard Protectors. PC, Macintosh.
> Hooleon Corporation   [61] $
>
> KeyGuard. 101-key keyboard templated to enhance keying accuracy.
> IBM Independence Series Information Center   [65] $

Keyguards
Prentke Romich Company   [102] $$

Unicorn Keyguards. Apple II.
Unicorn Engineering Inc.   [70] $

2.1b   Disk Guides—aid in the insertion of floppy disks into floppy drives.

Easy-Load-A-Diskette System
Extensions for Independence   [50] $

Disk Guide
Prentke Romich Company   [102] $

2.2   **Mouth Stick or Head Stick**—pointing devices that can be held in one's mouth or attached to a headband. Useful for pressing keys and buttons.

Adjustable Head Pointer
J. A. Preston Corp.   [73] $

2.3   **Augmentative Hand Devices**—pointing device that can be grasped in one's hand. Useful for accessing keyboards, telephones, etc.

Ableware Type Aid
Demco, Inc.   [33] $

2.4   **Page Turners**—enable individuals with limited hand or arm movement to more easily read books, magazines, and other texts.

Touch Turner. Page turning device. Battery-powered, operated by sensitive switches, turns magazines up to the size of *Life*, turns hardbound books up to the size of a volume of *World Book*. Turns pages either direction.
Touch Turner Company   [120] $

Deluxe Automatic Page Turner
J. A. Preston Corp.   [73] $$$$

2.5   **Door Knobs**—door handles are much easier to grasp than door knobs. There are also door handle adapters that fit over door knobs.

Leveron Door Knob Handle. Set of 2.
Demco, Inc.   [33] $

2.6 Alternative Computer Monitors

The Private Eye. Ultra-miniature display device to replace PC monitor. Allows user to move head while keeping image in focus. Comes with headset, operating manual, demonstration disk, and half-size IBM CGA interface board. Compatible with large-print software.
Reflection Technology, Inc.   [107] $$$$

2.7 Alternative Computer Input—a device that provides an alternative to the standard keyboard and mouse input.

2.7a Keyboard Enhancement Programs—software programs that enable slower typers to speed up and also adapt keyboards for efficient use with one hand.

KEYUP. Release information only when key is released, which prevents repeating when held down too long. PC.
Ability Systems Corp.   [1] $

Keyboard Configuration Software. PC.
ARTS Computer Products, Inc.   [16] $$$

FILCH. Keyboard control software.
Digital Equipment Corp.   [34] $$

Single Hand Keyboard System. IBM, Apple, or ADV.
In Touch Systems   [71] $$$$$

Keyboard Configuration/Accommodation Software. PC.
Kinetic Designs, Inc.   [76] $$

HandiSHIFT. Memory resident "sticky key" utility. Software and manual. PC.
Microsystems Software Inc.   [87] $

One Finger. PC, PS/2.
QuicKey
Trace Research and Development Center   [122] $; $

Dvorak One-Hand Keyboard. One-hand keyboard, either right or left hand; also available: IBM Selectric III for one hand. IBM PC, PS-2 or Apple IIe
Typewriting Institute for the Handicapped   [123] $$$$; $$$$$

27

Magic Fingers. Provides abbreviation expansion. PC.
Words+, Inc.   [134] $

2.7b   Keyboard Enhancement Hardware

PC Pedal. PC.
Brown & Company   [23] $

2.7c   Speech Recognition/Voice Input—high tech devices that are generally very expensive. Voice recognition input systems need to be customized to the individual user, and thus wouldn't be feasible for a library to provide this kind of system for patrons. However, there may be a need to acquire one for an employee who has constricted use of his/her limbs. Most voice recognition systems use macros as well as word prediction programming.

Dragon Dictate. Allows users to produce any free text by speaking instead of typing. 30,000 word vocabulary. Easy to use. Interactively learns the user's vocabulary. Compatible with most PC-based applications including word processing, database, and spreadsheet software. Can be adapted to an individual's pronunciation patterns which is a real benefit for an individual with a speech impairment. PC, PS/2.
Dragon Systems, Inc.   [37] $$$$$

Voice Navigator II. Speech recognition tool that works with Macintosh computers.
Articulate Systems Inc.   [15] $$$$

Voice Master Key System. PC, PS/2.
Covox, Inc.   [30] $$

Dragon Writer-1000. Speech recognition system. PC.
Dragon Systems, Inc.   [37] $$$$$

IBM VoiceType. Speech recognition system with 7,000 word vocabulary and word prediction (made possible with 80,000 word dictionary). PC.
Dragon Systems, Inc. (IBM is an authorized remarketer)   [37] $$$$$

IBM PC Voice Activated Keyboard Utility
IBM Independence Series Information Center   [65] $$$

28

Speech Recognition Keyboard. PC.
Key Tronic Corp.   [75] $$$$

Pronounce. Speech input system. Includes microphone, circuit
    card, and software. PC.
MTI, Inc. [40] $$$$

Speech Recognition System. PC.
Scott Instruments Corp.   [109] $$$$$

IntroVoice VI, V. PC.
Voice Connection   [130] $$$$

Micro IntroVoice. PC.
Voice Connection   [130] $$$$$

Voice Card. PC.
Votan, a division of MOSCOM Corp.   [131] $$$$$

Speech Recognition System. PC.
Words+, Inc. [134] $$$$$

2.7d Alternative Keyboards—non-traditional alphanumeric keyboards
    designed for individuals who have difficulty typing on a standard
    keyboard.

Smartboard. Programmable keyboard for PC/XT and compatibles.
ARTS Computer Products, Inc.   [16] $$

FreeWheel System Model 1. Infrared typing and head pointing
    input system. Includes camera, cables, FreeBoard software,
    FreeWheel driver, reflector kit, manual, tutor program. PC,
    Macintosh, Apple II.
Digital Equipment Corp.   [34] $$$$$

KB 5153 Touch Pad Keyboard. PC.
Key Tronic Corp.   [75] $$

Eyegaze Computer Systems. Includes IBM 386 computer.
LC Technologies, Inc.   [79] $$$$$

HeadMaster. Alternative to keyboard and mouse. Head movements direct the cursor on the screen. Sip & puff switch controls the clicking of the mouse. An on-screen keyboard is also incorporated. Macintosh, IBM.
Prentke Romich Company   [102] $$$$$

EyeTyper 300. Eye controlled input system. Apple II, PC.
Sentient Systems Technology, Inc.   [111] $$$$$

One Hand Computer Keyboards. Apple II, PC, PS/2.
Typewriting Institute for the Handicapped   [123] $$$$

2.7e   Larger (or Expanded) Keyboards—typically touch-sensitive membrane surface divided into squares representing keys. Some models have the ability to reprogram the position of the keys.

Keyport 300. PC.
Polytel Computer Products, Inc.   [100] $$

Configurable Membrane Keyboard to augment functions of standard keyboard. PC.
Polytel Computer Products, Inc.   [100] $$

IntelliKeys. Touch-sensitive squares. Valuable to people with physical as well as visual disabilities. Comes with 7 overlays and 576 programmable keys that can be grouped to form larger keys.
Unicorn Engineering, Inc.   [70] $$$

Unicorn Membrane Keyboards. Apple II, Macintosh, PC.
Unicorn Engineering, Inc.   [70] $$$

Expanded Keyboard Emulator. PC.
Words+ Inc.   [134] $$$$

2.7f   Smaller Keyboards—recommended for users with a limited range of motion in their hands, wrists, or arms.

Mini Keyboard
Don Johnston, Inc.   [35] $$$

Twiddler. Pocket-sized mouse pointer plus full-function keyboard
in single unit that fits into one hand. Compatible with DOS or
Microsoft Windows 3.0. Parks on velcro patch on side of monitor. No mouse pad or desktop is needed.
Handykey Corporation   [56] $$

Magic Wand Keyboard. Miniature full-function computer keyboard
that works with touch of either handheld wand or mouthstick
wand. Compatible with Apple IIgs and Macintosh and IBM
(and compatible) computers.
In Touch Systems   [71] $$$$$

Keyport 60. PC.
Polytel Computer Products Corp.   [100] $$

The Unicorn Mini Keyboard. PC.
Unicorn Engineering, Inc.   [70] $$

2.7g   Touch Screens—user inputs information into the computer by
touching commands on the screen. Valuable for users who have dif-
ficulty accessing a standard keyboard or a mouse.

Touch System
Carroll Touch, Inc.   [25] $$$$ Controller $$

TouchWINDOW. Provides touch input access to most software
applications that require a mouse. Requires Adaptive Firmware
Card. Versions available for Apple II, Macintosh, and PCs.
Edmark Corporation   [43] $$$

UNMOUSE. Macintosh.
MicroTouch Systems, Inc.   [88] $$

2.7h   Mouse Entry—alternative to standard computer mouse entry which
moves the cursor around the screen in the same way.

Trackball. Includes microspeed PC Trac serial pointing device with
software driver. Input option is available for FreeBoard.
Digital Equipment Corp.   [34] $$

Mouse-Trak. Trackball mouse emulation.
Itac Systems, Inc.   [72] $$

PC-TRAC, MacTRAC.
MicroSpeed, Inc.   [86] $$

Standard Headmaster, Remote Headmaster. Headset and control
    unit allow movement of mouse pointer on screen. Includes puff
    switch to operate standard mouse button. Apple IIgs, Macintosh,
    or IBM; remote operates on infrared link (up to 12 feet).
Prentke Romich Company   [102] $$$$$

PowerMouse 100
ProHance Technologies   [104] $$

2.7i   Joystick Entry—identical to the kind of joystick used in many video
        games, this kind of device allows a user to navigate around a key-
        board like a mouse.

    LipStick. Joystick typing and pointing device. Macintosh.
    MacIntyre Computer Systems Division   [84] $$$

    PRC Joystick. Pushing the handle in any of four directions will acti-
        vate a switch.
    Prentke Romich Company   [102] $$

2.7j   Interface Card/Hardware and Software—the components needed to
        make alternative input devices work with standard computer soft-
        ware. Typically switch interfaces connect to the computer through
        the game port.

    PC Serial AID. PC.
    Don Johnston, Inc.   [35] $$$

    Ke:nx 2.0. Interface box used between Macintosh and wide variety
        of alternative input devices including scanners, alternate key-
        boards, assisted keyboards and morse code input.
    Don Johnston, Inc.   [35] $$$$

    CINTEX. Multi-function interface between personal computer and
        adaptive input devices. PC.
    NanoPac, Inc.   [90] $$$$$

2.7k   On-Screen Keyboards—useful for patrons or employees who are
        unable to type on a standard keyboard. On-screen keyboards can be
        accessed with a variety of switch-based input devices.

Proportional Keystroke Scanner. Used with sip & puff systems. PC, PS/2 models 25/30 and 50/60.
Ability Systems Corp.   [1] $$$$$

ScanPAC w/RealVoice
Adaptive Communication Systems   [6] $$$$$

ScreenKeys. Macintosh. Accessory keyboard in movable, size adjustable window.
Berkeley Systems   [20] $

WordWriter. Compatible with all Macintosh applications, including HyperCard.
MacIntyre Computer Systems Division   [84] $$

HandiKEY. PC, PS/2.
HandiKEY Deluxe
Microsystems Software Inc.   [87] $$$; $$$$

FreeBoard. Software-based keyboard emulator. Includes FreeBoard software, joystick driver, manual and tutor program.
Manufactured by Digital Equipment Corp.
Pointer Systems   [99] $$$$$

WiViK. For Microsoft Windows 3.0. Works with any mouse device; personalized keyboards can be created.
Prentke Romich Company   [102] $$

2.71   Word Processing Programs—user friendly word processing software designed for users with disabilities.

WriteAway. Features provide rate enhancement, speech output, spelling assistance, and multiple access modes. Input can be from standard keyboard, assisted keyboard, or built-in scanning. Includes word prediction and word completion, macro capability. Switch interface with hardware.
Institute on Applied Technology   [68] $$

Abbreviation/Expansion. Apple IIe.
ZYGO Industries, Inc.   [136] $

2.7m Morse Code Software—allows morse code input, from among a variety of switches, to be translated to alphanumeric characters. Many programs have word prediction capability.

MorseK. PC, PS/2.
Kinetic Designs, Inc.   [76] $$

HandiCODE. Memory resident morse code input via any single switch interface or morse code paddle. When connected with voice synthesizer, it can be used for voice output. Runs with MS-DOS. Software, manual, switch connector, and port connector. PC, PS/2.
HandiCODE DELUXE includes HandiWORD word prediction/abbreviation software.
Microsystems Software Inc.   [87] $$$; $$$$

2.7n Switches—enable use of a computer without using a keyboard or mouse. Wide variety: sip & puff, head/finger/arm/wrist control, etc. Mostly recommended for employees. In most cases, switch configurations are customized to the individual.

Ablenet, Inc.   [3] $
Creative Switch Industries   [31] $$
Don Johnston, Inc.   [35] $
DU-IT Control Systems Group, Inc.   [38] $$
Luminaud, Inc.   [81] $
Nassau Applied Technology Resource Center   [125] $
Prentke Romich Company   [102] $
Tapeswitch Corp.   [115] $
TASH, Inc.   [116] $$
ZYGO Industries, Inc.   [136] $$

2.8 **Optimal Positioning**—Conventional tables and seating can be awkward and uncomfortable for patrons with physical impairments to use when reading, writing, or using a computer. These devices allow the user to adjust the physical environment to better suit his or her range of motion.

Gore Reading Stand. Aluminum and steel.
American Printing House for the Blind   [10] $

Slant Boards. Small (24" x 19"); large (30" x 27").
Attainment Company, Inc.   [18] $$; $$$$

Slim Armstrong. Telescoping arm switch mounting system that is flexible, strong, and easy to use.
Ablenet, Inc.   [3] $$

Full Flex Valet. Computer monitor extension arm with various mounts.
Demco, Inc.   [33] $$

Adjustable Workstation
Demco, Inc.   [33] $$$

Ableware Roberts Book Holder
Demco, Inc.   [33] $

Miller Deluxe Book Holder
J. A. Preston Corp.   [73] $

Hold and Read Book Holder
Demco, Inc.   [33] $

Newspaper Holder with Holder Base
Demco, Inc.   [33] $$

Adjustable Low Vision Reading Stand
Exceptional Teaching Aids   [49] $

3.0 FOR LOW VISION

3.1   **Large Character Display**—products for increasing the size of alphanumeric characters to be more easily read by individuals with vision impairments. Large character display devices are also useful for individuals with learning disabilities.

3.1a   Large Button Telephone

Big Button Telephone
AT&T Accessible Communications Product Center   [17] $

3.1b   Large Print Typewriter

Large Type Typewriter. 6 spaces to the inch horizontally (versus 10
       and 12 for pica and elite), 4 vertical lines to the inch (versus 6
       for pica and elite)
Typewriting Institute for the Handicapped   [123] $$$$

3.1c   Computer Keyboards—labels and keycaps with larger alphanumeric
       characters to be put over standard keytops.

Touchdown KeyTop/KeyFront Kits
Hooleon Corporation   [61] $

ZoomCaps Key Labels
Don Johnston, Inc.   [35] $

3.1d   Software—memory resident software that enlarges the text of other
       software being used.

In Focus
Ai Squared   [8] $$

Magnim GT. Software-based screen magnifier, up to 10x. Thick
       high resolution characters.
Artic Technologies International, Inc.   [14] $$$$

PC Lens. Software that enlarges text 5x to 20x on screen. PC, XT,
       AT.
ARTS Computer Products, Inc.   [16] $$$

Large Print for Dot Matrix Printer. PC. Large print for Mac printer.
       Macintosh.
ARTS Computer Products, Inc.   [16] $$; $

Large Print Display Software. Apple II, Macintosh.
Berkeley Systems, Inc.   [20] $

Stepping Out II (up to 16x) for Macs.
Berkeley Systems, Inc.   [20] $$

MAGic (1.2x, 1.4x, and 2x). PC.
Microsystems Software Inc.   [87] $

MAGic Deluxe (up to 12x). PC.
Microsystems Software Inc.   [87] $$

inLARGE. Magnifying software 2x to 16x, characters and graphics.
    Macintosh.
Berkeley Systems, Inc.   [20] $

Large Print Production Software. Enlarges text when printed with
    dot matrix printer.
Enabling Technologies Company   [46] $$$$

Large-Type Word Processing Program. Allows printing in standard
    or large type.
National Institute for Rehabilitation Engineering   [92] $$

LP-DOS Version 5.0 Magnifying Software. Supports Microsoft
    Windows and MS-DOS applications. Magnifies up to 16x. PC,
    PS/2.
Optelec US, Inc.   [95] $$$$

ZoomText 4.0. Character magnification, 2x to 8x, 4 fonts, may be
    split into two windows—horizontally or vertically, scrolling and
    tracking, menu-driven, compatible with most character-based
    software, requires EGA card in computer. PC, XT, AT, PS/2.
ZoomText Plus
Raised-Dot Computing, Inc.   [105] $$$; $$$$

Fancy Font. Large print for dot matrix printers. PC.
Softcraft, Inc.   [113] $$

Soft Vista. PC.
Telesensory Corp.   [118] $$$$$

3.1e   Copying Machine with Enlarging—most major copying machine
    manufacturers have models with enlarging capabilities.

Selectec BookMaster 1801. Copying machine with foot pedal, large
    capacity paper cassette, topless feature with retina shield.
University Copy Services, Inc.   [126] $$$$$

3.1f Magnifying Lenses for Reading Print Materials—standard handheld and desk models.

BOSSERT Specialties, Inc. [22] $

3.1g Magnifying Lens for Computer Monitor—an external lens that fits on the front of the computer monitor.

Compu-Lenz. Fresnel lens screen magnifier (2x-4x) and screen filter. Fits PC and compatible sizes.
Florida New Concepts, Inc. [52] $$

Beamscope II
Florida New Concepts, Inc. [52] $

3.1h Magnifying Lens for Television Screen

Vidcon
Florida New Concepts, Inc. [52] $$

3.1i Closed Circuit TV Systems (CCTV)—closed circuit television systems are used to electronically magnify printed text, maps, diagrams, objects, etc. A video camera is mounted pointing at a copy stand where the material to be viewed is placed. A magnifying zoom lens enables the user to magnify the image to a range of sizes. Black-and-white and color magnification systems are both available.

Viewscan. Portable large print reading device with hand scan camera; Viewscan Text System adds a notetaker/word processor.
HumanWare, Inc. [64] $$$$$

Chroma CCD (color); Lynx—CCD display on computer monitor; (also Automated Viewing Table).
Telesensory Corp. [118] $$$$$

Large Print Display System; CCTV systems—Vantage CCD; Voyager CCD; Voyager XL CCD; Chroma CCD (color); Miniature Electronic Visual Aid (MEVA) System; Computer magnification systems—Vista (color text and graphics magnification system for PC and P/S2 computers and compatibles); Lynx (transports video image into computer screen); Large Print Display Processor—magnifies up to 16x, models available compatible with PC, PS/2, and Apple II computers.
Telesensory Corp. [118] $$$$$

4.0 FOR BLINDNESS

4.1 Braille Writing and Embossing Equipment—braille "typewriters."

> Perkins Brailler. Capable of embossing 25 lines of 41 cells each. Aluminum framework with baked enamel finish. High-impact plastic keys, knobs, and carriage.
> American Printing House for the Blind, Inc.   [10] $$$$

4.2 Braille Input Devices—braille-making keyboards that produce code that is translated into computer text.

> Notex. Refreshable braille display and portable braille notetaker. Rechargeable battery. Can be connected to serial port of most computers to transfer files. 24-cell or 40-cell display. PC.
> Adhoc Reading Systems   [7] $$$$$

> APH PocketBraille. Portable notetaking device with speech output. Built-in braille keyboard. Can import to or export from a computer. Optional add-on memory unit.
> American Printing House for the Blind   [10] $$$$

> Braille Note-Taker and Terminal. Apple II, Macintosh, PC.
> Blazie Engineering, Inc.   [21] $$$$

> Braille'n Speak Package System. Portable talking device with a calculator, carrying case, and an interfacing kit; Braille'n Speak Disk Drive Accessory—battery-powered floppy disk drive 3.5". Provides portable MS-DOS-compatible storage for Braille'n Speak Package System.
> Digital Equipment Corp.   [34] $$$$$; $$$

> BrailleMate. Pocket computer with braille keyboard, speech synthesizer and braille cell for speech and braille output. Stores up to 128 pages of braille with expandable memory capacity. Data can be printed, embossed or copied to another computer.
> Telesensory Corp.   [118] $$$$$

4.3 **Keyboards/Keytops**—accessories to help the blind user locate keys on the computer keyboard.

> Braille Keyboard Overlay for Apple IIgs.
> American Printing House for the Blind   [10]
>
> Loc-Dots. Clear adhesive keyboard dots.
> ARTS Computer Products, Inc.   [16] $
>
> High Dots. Spongy adhesive-backed dots. 112 small, 48 medium,
>   and 32 large.
> Exceptional Teaching Aids   [49] $
>
> Braille Keytop Labels
> Hooleon Corporation   [61] $

4.4 **Braille Output Devices**—the two most common types of braille output devices are paperless braille displays and braille printer/embossers. Paperless braille displays are most useful for blind computer users who are using word processing, spreadsheets, or other commercial software. They merely need the means for "looking" at the screen. Braille printer/embossers are used more for printing final documents, either those that have been composed by the user or those that the user has transferred from computer text to braille.

> 4.4a Screen Access/Paperless Braille Displays—braille output devices that enable blind users to navigate computer screens. Smooth-tipped pins electronically pop up or retract to create the braille characters of whatever word or line is highlighted on the screen.
>
> > Braille Screen Review System, Magga Package. PC.
> > Enabling Technologies Company   [46] $$$
> >
> > KeyBraille. Braille display positioned on front edge of KeyBraille. 5
> >   separate braille cells constantly display line, column and special
> >   attribute information. 20-cell or 40-cell reading display. PC.
> > HumanWare, Inc.   [64] $$$$$
> >
> > Navigator. 20 braille character, 6-dot desktop unit; 40 braille char-
> >   acter, 8-dot unit; 80 character, 8-dot unit. PC.
> > Telesensory Corp.   [118] $$$$$; $$$$$+

Optacon II. Allows individuals who cannot see to feel the visual information instead. A small camera passes across the screen and transmits what it views to a small bed of vibrating pins. The user places fingertips on the bed to determine the shape of the images on the screen. inTOUCH software interfaces with Optacon II to provide tactile and large screen access for the Macintosh. Optacon PC software (and mouse) provides tactile access to the PC or PS/2 screen.
Telesensory Corp.   [118] $$$$$

Braille Screen Review System. Compatible with all computing systems.
Telesensory Corp.   [118] $$$$$

4.5   **Braille Translation Software (from print to braille)**—this software converts computer text to braille code for use with paperless braille devices and braille printer/embossers.

PC Braille. Software that translates text files to grade 1, 2, or computer braille formats. PC.
ARTS Computing Products, Inc.   [16] $$$

PC Sift. PC.
ARTS Computer Products, Inc.   [16] $$

Duxbury Braille Translator. Text-to-braille and braille-to-text translation program. Allows sighted person with no knowledge of braille to type, edit, and format into braille. Apple II, PC.
Duxbury Systems, Inc.   [39] $$$

Braille Translation Software. Apple II, PC.
Enabling Technologies Company   [46] $$

Braille Translation Software
Intelligent Information Technologies   [69] $$

Turbo Braille. Translates and formats braille from WordPerfect, WordStar, or ASCII text sources.
Auto Braille
Kansys, Inc.   [74] $$$; $

Hot Dots Version 3.0. Menu-driven braille translation from standard text to grade 2 braille and vice versa. PC.
Raised Dot Computing   [105] $$$

NFBTRANS. Translation from text to grade 2 braille. Embosser or paperless braille producer is required. PC.
Roudley Associates, Inc.   [108] $$

MPrint. Connects to a Perkins Brailler and translates grade 2 braille characters into standard alphabetic characters for standard printing.
Telesensory Corp.   [118] $$$$

4.6   Braille Printers/Embossers—instead of printing with ink, braille printer/embossers press braille dots onto the paper. Some models are capable of both ink printing and braille embossing simultaneously.

Ohtsuki BT-5000 Printer. Produces parallel lines of braille and standard ink print simultaneously. Compatible with most computers including IBM, Apple, and Macintosh. Ohtsuki Communications.
American Thermoform Corp.   [11] $$$$$

Braillon Thermoform Duplicator. For copying brailled or embossed materials.
American Thermoform Corp.   [11] $$$$$

ATC/Resus 214 Printer. 210 lines per minute of 6-dot braille. Also capable of printing 8-dot braille.
American Thermoform Corp.   [11] $$$$$+

Braillo 40 and Braillo 90. 40 and 90 characters per second (cps). Manually switchable from 6- to 8-point braille (model 40; model 90).
American Thermoform Corp.   [11] $$$$$

Index Braille Printer.
ARTS Computer Products, Inc.   [16] $$$$$

Braille Blazer. Braille embosser with synthesized speech output. Small, light, quiet. Prints at speed of 10 to 15 characters per

second. Uses convenient 8-1/2" x 11" braille paper. Works with
   most screen review software. Compatible with all computers.
Blazie Engineering, Inc.   [21] $$$$$

Juliet Brailler. A desk-top printer that accepts paper of any weight
   (20–100 pounds) and can handle 15-inch wide paper and repro-
   duce on both sides of the page.
Enabling Technologies Company   [46] $$$$$

Romeo Braille Printer 20 and Marathon Brailler are among a variety
   of personal and production capacity braille embossers available.
   Compatible with all computers.
Enabling Technologies Company   [46] $$$$$+

Index Braille Printers. PC.
HumanWare, Inc.   [64] $$$$$+

Braille-n-Print. Produces grade 2 braille and typed text from a
   Perkins Brailler.
HumanWare, Inc.   [64] $$$$$

Everest-DT Braille Embosser. High speed interpoint (double-sided)
   embosser that reproduces braille text and graphics. Prints on
   single sheets of braille paper. Works with OsCaR.
Telesensory Corp.   [118] $$$$$

VersaPoint-40. PC.
Telesensory Corp.   [118] $$$$$

4.7   **Text-to-Speech Synthesizers**—internal and external voice synthesizers are
used to translate computer text to spoken words.

   4.7a   Internal Synthesizers—peripheral card is inserted into the computer
   and provides voice output. No external devices are required.

   Accent-PC. Can speak in two modes: Text and Spell. 60-850 words
      per minute speech rate. PC.
   Aicom Corporation   [9] $$$$

   SynPhonix 210, 220, 230, 240
   Artic Technologies International, Inc.   [14] $$$$

43

outSPOKEN. The Talking Macintosh Interface. Software that translates visual information on screen to audible information.
Berkeley Systems, Inc.   [20] $$$

Prose 4000
Centigram Communications Corp.   [26] $$$$$

Listen for Windows. Includes software and 8-bit ISA sound recognition card and headset microphone. Can handle about 300 active words.
Verben   [127] $$$$

4.7b External Synthesizers/Speakers—usually a self-contained "add-on" component. Some models will require text-to-speech translation software. Typically includes the synthesizer and a connecting cable.

Echo II. Synthesized voice access to standard commercial computer software, includes circuit card, external speaker box, and TEXTALKER software. Volume and rate control, headphone jack for Apple computers.
American Printing House for the Blind   [10] $$

Speaqualizer. Hardware attachment that allows user to hear any text running on an IBM PC-compatible operating system. It includes a control box with speaker, a card to fit into a computer expansion slot, and a connecting cable. Volume, rate of speech, and pitch are adjustable. Also type spoken echo. PC, PS/2 model 30.
American Printing House for the Blind   [10] $$$$

Artic Crystal. PC.
Artic Technologies International, Inc.   [14] $$$$

DECtalk. Voice synthesizer compatible with many computers. 9 different voices, converts text using pronunciation code, dictionary, and letter-to-sound rules. 120-350 wpm. Apple II, PC.
Digital Equipment Corp.   [34] $$$$$

MultiVoice. Based on Digital's DECtalk technology. Portable and battery-powered. Can be used with most available microcomputers.
Institute on Applied Technology   [68] $$$$$

44

Intex-Talker. Keyboard speech output system. Apple II, PC.
Microsystems Software   [87] $$$

Audapter Speech System. Speech output, up to 500 wpm, no soft-
    ware required.
Personal Data Systems   [96] $$$$$

Echo II, Echo PC. Packaged with either TEXTALKER or
    TEXTALKERgs (for Apple IIgs) software.
Street Electronics Corp.   [42] $$

4.8   **Text-to-Speech Software for Synthesizers**—software that converts computer text to speech code to be used with a speech synthesizer.

TEXTALKER (for ProDOS and DOS 3.3) and TEXTALKERgs (for
    Apple IIgs). These programs allow most text-based software pro-
    grams to speak. Pitch, volume, rate of speech, and other charac-
    teristics of speech can be controlled from the keyboard. Must
    be used in conjunction with a speech synthesizer. TEXTALKER
    software only works with ECHO speech synthesizers.
American Printing House for the Blind   [10] $

Vision Business. PC.
Artic Technologies International, Inc.   [14] $$$$

PC Voice. Text-to-speech software, compatible speech synthesizer
    required. PC and MS DOS.
ARTS Computer Products, Inc.   [16] $$$$

Verbal Operating System. PC, PS/2.
Computer Conversations   [27] $$$$

Reading Software and Synthesizer. Enable Reader public domain
    software; screen reading software: VP. PC.
Enabling Technologies Company   [46] $$$$$

JAWS (Jobs Access With Speech). Pop-up menus, macros, windows,
    dual cursors. Screenreading software for use with voice synthe-
    sizer (not included). Includes both 5.25" and 3.5" disks. PC,
    PS/2.
Henter-Joyce, Inc.   [59] $$$

45

IBM PS/2 Screen Reader. 3278 emulation screen reading software. Works with standard software, requires special keypad for screen navigating, windowing capability. Includes keypad, software, and documentation. Speech synthesizer required but not included. PS/2.
IBM Independence Series Information Center   [65] $$$$$

Provox. Voice output software. Requires external synthesizer, works with 5 different models. PC.
Kansys, Inc.   [74] $$$$

Flipper 3.0. Voice output screen access, requires MS-DOS or PC-DOS 2.1 or later. Works with a variety of voice synthesizers. PC.
Raised Dot Computing, Inc.   [105] $$$

Screen Reading System. Software; synthesizer.
Personal Data Systems, Inc.   [96] $$$$

Screen Reading Software. Apple II, PC.
Raised Dot Computing   [105] $$

SoftVert 3278 Vert, VertPlus speech access software. PC.
Telesensory Corp.   [118] $$$

EZ Keys. Text-to-speech output to augment communication. PC.
Words+, Inc.   [134] $$$$$

4.9   **Optical Character Scanner**—device used for sweeping across printed page to transfer alphanumeric characters to computer readable format so they can be speech synthesized, turned into braille, or otherwise electronically manipulated.

Adhoc Reader. Capable of scanning sheet of text so it may be read using a speech synthesizer. Scans up to 8-1/2" x 14" page, 6–14 pt. type. Includes DocuRead scanning software. Model 200 reads single sheets only. Model 400 reads single sheets and bound documents. IBM XT/AT or compatible with 640K memory and hard drive.
Adhoc Reading Systems   [7] $$$

Handy Scan. Scanner that can direct output to an internal speech synthesizer. PC.
Adhoc Reading Systems   [7] $$$

Desktop Scanner. PC, PS/2.
IBM Independence Series Information Center   [65] $$$$

Personal Reader. Standalone optical reader that reads text and converts it into DECtalk synthetic speech. Model 7315-10 (includes handheld scanner); Model 7315-20 (includes automatic scanner); Model 7315-30 (includes both types of scanners).
Kurzweil Applied Intelligence, Inc.   [78] $$$$$; $$$$$; $$$$$+

4.10 **Optical Character Recognition (OCR) Systems**—systems and devices that can "read" printed text aloud or can translate that information into a computer file so it can be translated into braille.

DocuRead Expert. Intelligent reader operates with variety of scanners, computers, and adaptive output devices. Menu-driven, recognizes over 20,000 type styles between 6 and 28 point size. Includes HP ScanJet Plus Scanner, Scanner Interface (daughter card), Truescan Model E, and DocuRead IDB Software. PC, PS/; DocuRead IDB software only.
Adhoc Reading Systems   [7] $$$$$; $$$

Boxer Reader-286. 19 lb. computer with character recognition system and hand scanner. Includes 286 computer, hand scanner, Truescan Model E, Letter Perfect, Reader Package, Synphonix 215 with Artic Vision, Hand Scanner Interface Card, DocuRead IDB Software, Encore and carry bag. Same components with 386 computer.
Adhoc Reading Systems   [7] $$$$$

Arkenstone Reader II. Integrated optical character recognition (OCR) system that creates and prints machine-readable files, compatible with speech synthesizers, braille displays, and braille printers. Includes TrueScan, scanner recognition card (from Calera Recognition Systems); ScanJet Plus desktop scanner (from Hewlett-Packard); and Arkenstone Reader II software. PC/AT, PS/2.
Arkenstone, Inc.   [13] $$$$$

47

Arkenstone Hand Scanner. Can scan a page up to 8-1/2" wide and
    14" long. With Arkenstone Reader II software, it can be used to
    read with a voice synthesizer or braille device. Includes scanner,
    driver software update, and interface card.
    Arkenstone, Inc.   [13] $$$$

Eyes. PC.
    ARTS Computer Products, Inc.   [16] $$$$$

OsCaR. PC, PS/2.
    Telesensory Corp.   [118] $$$$$

4.11 Other Devices and Tools

Relief Maps and Globes
    American Printing House for the Blind   [10] $

Clock Face with Raised Print and Braille Numbers
    American Printing House for the Blind   [10] $

CHAPTER 3

Vendors/ Manufacturers

Cay Gasque

1. **Ability Systems Corporation**
    1422 Arnold Avenue
    Roslyn, PA 19001

    Tel. (215) 657-4338

    Comment: Manufactures and sells the Proportional Keystroke Scanner, a keyboard emulator with sip & puff control, and Key-up software, which enters keystroke on upstroke of key only.

    Disabilities: physical

2. **The AbleTech Connection**
    P. O. Box 898
    Westerville, OH 43081

    Tel. (614) 899-9989
    (800) 589-8835 Ohio only

    Comment: Sells the Compu-Lenz, a fresnel lens which attaches to the computer monitor and enlarges the display. Requires no wiring or power source. Also distributes Ultratec TDDs and is exclusive distributor in Ohio for Telesensory low vision products.

    Disabilities: low vision, learning, hearing

3. **Ablenet, Inc.**
    1081 10th Avenue SE
    Minneapolis, MN 55414-1312

    Tel. (800) 322-0956
    (612) 379-0956
    Fax (612) 379-9143

    Comment: Develops, manufactures, and distributes a variety of products including switches, environmental control units, mounting systems, adapters and communication devices, including Big Red, Jelly Bean Switch, and Slim Armstrong mounting system. A full catalog of products is available. Also offers referral and information services.

    Disabilities: physical, mental

4. H. Abraham and Associates
2535 Seminole
Detroit, MI 48214-1855

Tel. (313) 925-9368
Fax (313) 925-3593

Comment: Factory regional representative/reseller for Xerox Imaging Systems/Kurzweil scanning products, Artic Technologies speech and large print products, Celexx CCTVs. Sells various other products including braille translators, large print software, computers, etc. Importer of Index Braille printers for wholesale distribution.

Disabilities: low vision, blindness, learning, hearing impaired

5. Access Unlimited
3535 Briarpark Drive
Suite 102
Houston, TX 77042-5325

Tel. (800) 848-0311
    (713) 781-7441
Fax (713) 781-3550

Comment: Access Unlimited disseminates information on a wide variety of adaptive technology products and markets over 800 customized or adapted computer devices and software. Products include speech synthesizers for MS-DOS, Macintosh and Apple II, and compatible software, switches, expanded keyboards and overlays, speech and large print software, educational software, alternative input devices, computer headphone sets. Access Unlimited also provides technical support training workshops and consultation services. Services are geared to youth.

Disabilities: physical, learning, low vision, blindness, mental retardation, hearing, deafness

6. ACS Technologies, Inc.
(formerly Adaptive Communication Systems, Inc.)
1400 Lee Drive
Coraopolis, PA 15108-1292

Tel. (800) 117-2922
    (412) 269-6656
Fax (412) 269-6675

Comment: Manufactures and sells a variety of communication aids for physically impaired, especially speech impaired. Products include speech synthesizers, environmental control switches and devices, alternative keyboards, keyboard enhancements, and voice- and eye-operated switching devices. Examples of products: Real Voice, Real Voice PC, ACS Twinkle Remote switch.

Disabilities: physical, learning, speech

Adaptive Communication Systems
See 6, ACS Technologies, Inc.

7. Adhoc Reading Systems
228 E. 85th Street
Suite 12B
New York, NY 10028

Tel. (212) 717-4835
Fax (212) 717-4835

Comment: Develops, integrates and distributes hardware and software for visually impaired. Products include optical character recognition reading machines that convert text to speech; can be used with adaptive output device to produce braille, large print, or speech. Products can be used with IBM computers.

Disabilities: low vision, blindness

8. Ai Squared

P.O. Box 669
Manchester Center, VT
05255-0669

Tel. (802) 362-3612
Fax (802) 362-1670

Comment: Produces, sells, and distributes to dealers for sale, large print display software for IBM PC and compatibles. Product names: Zoomtext, Zoomtext Plus, inFocus. Also sells VisAbility, a software program that uses a scanner and a PC to create a reading system.

Disabilities: low vision, learning disabled

9. Aicom Corporation

1590 Oakland Road
Suite B112
San Jose, CA 95131

Tel. (408) 453-8251
Fax (408) 453-8255

Comment: Manufactures, sells and distributes to dealers for sale, the Accent speech synthesizer; available in both external and internal models for IBM PC and compatibles, IBM PS/2 and Toshiba computers. The external unit can be used with Macintosh and Apple II.

Disabilities: low vision, blindness, learning, speech

American Communication Corporation

See 41, Eastern Electronics Corp.

10. American Printing House for the Blind

1839 Frankfort Avenue
P.O. Box 6058
Louisville, KY 40206

Tel. (800) 223-1839
(502) 895-2405
Fax (502) 895-1509

Comment: Manufactures books and magazines in braille, large type, recorded and computer disk format. Also manufactures a variety of educational and daily living aids, such as braille paper and styluses, talking book equipment and synthetic speech computer products. APH also offers CARL ET AL, an electronic database that lists braille, large type and recorded textbooks available from companies across the U.S. Also offers two free newsletters, *APH Slate* (a general newsletter) and *Micro Materials Update* (a newsletter on computer products).

Disabilities: low vision, blindness

11. American Thermoform Corp.

2311 Travers Avenue
City of Commerce, CA 90040

Tel. (800) 331-3676
(213) 723-9021
Fax (213) 728-8877

Comment: Manufactures and sells Thermoform machine and distributes braille printers and computer braille paper.

Disabilities: blindness

12. APR Computer Technology

(formerly Index Braille Printer Co.)
4420 Norledge Street
Kansas City, MO 64123

Tel. (800) 421-9775
    (816) 363-5817
Fax (816) 483-8869

Comment: Distributor of software and hardware products for blind individuals and those with low vision, including braille interface for IBM and compatible computers. Also sells screen enlargers with speech, Accent voice synthesizers, Zoomtext software.

Disabilities: blindness, low vision

13. Arkenstone, Inc.

1390 Borregas Avenue
Sunnyvale, CA 94089

Tel. (800) 444-4443
    (408) 752-2200
Fax (408) 745-6739

Comment: Manufacturer. Principal product is Arkenstone reading machine and software for the machine. Sells Hewlett Packard desk scanners with machine.

Disabilities: low vision, blindness, dyslexia, learning

14. Artic Technologies International, Inc.

55 Park Street
Suite 2
Troy, MI 48083-2753

Tel. (313) 588-7370
    (800) 677-3848 for technical support only; not for product information

Fax (313) 588-2650

Comment: Manufactures and sells through distributors (no direct sales) speech synthesizers (Artic TransPort external and battery-operated), screen enlarging software, speech output software, and accessories. Also offers training and technical support.

Disabilities: low vision, blindness

15. Articulate Systems Inc.

600 West Cummings Park
Suite 4500
Woburn, MA 01801

Tel. (800) 443-7077
    (617) 935-5656
    (617) 935-2220 for technical support
Fax (617) 935-0490

Comment: Develops and manufactures voice input devices for computer software and hardware for Macintosh computers.

Disabilities: physical

16. ARTS Computer Products, Inc.

33 Richdale Avenue
Suite 228
Cambridge, MA 02140

Tel. (800) 343-0095
    (617) 547-5320

Comment: Manufactures augmentative products and sells them direct and through distributors. Also sells products of other manufacturers. Products include reading machines, braille printers, keyboard enhancements, speech output software, screen reading software, large print display and output, and braille translation software.

Disabilities: low vision, blindness, mobility, physical, learning

17. AT & T Accessible Communications Product Center
5 Wood Hollow Road
Suite 1119
Parsippany, NJ 07054

Tel. (800) 233-1222 voice and TDD
Fax (201) 581-3972

Comment: Sells adaptive products for hearing, sight and mobility impairments, including amplification handsets, telephone aids, TDDs, tone ringers, flashing signals, big button telephones, speaker phones, cordless phones. Also provides a referral service for products not available from AT & T.

Disabilities: hearing, deafness, low vision, mobility, physical

18. Attainment Company, Inc.
504 Commerce Parkway
Verona, WI 53593-1377

Tel. (800) 327-4269
      (608) 845-7880
Fax (608) 845-8040

Comment: Manufactures multi-media life skill materials for people who don't read, including adults with developmental disabilities, head injuries, strokes, non-readers or non-English speaking individuals. Topics include shopping, personal care, meal planning, communication, budgeting, community activities, etc. A free catalog of products is available (request Catalog '94L).

Disabilities: learning, mental

19. AVR Technologies, Inc.
(formerly Advanced Vision Research, Inc.)
71 East Daggett Drive
San Jose, CA 95134

Tel. (800) 544-6243
      (408) 434-1115
Fax (408) 434-0968

Comment: Manufactures flat bed image scanners for Macintosh and PC computers.

Disabilities: low vision

20. Berkeley Systems, Inc.
2095 Rose Street
Berkeley, CA 94709

Tel. (510) 540-5535
      (800) 344-5541 for orders
      only
Fax (510) 540-5115

Comment: Produces screen enlarging and speech output software for the Macintosh computer. Also sells screen saver program.

Disabilities: low vision, blindness, learning

21. Blazie Engineering, Inc.
105 E. Jarrettsville Road
Forest Hill, MD 21050

Tel. (410) 893-9333
Fax (410) 836-5040

Comment:: Manufactures and sells Braille Blazer Portable braille embosser/speech synthesizer, Braille 'n Speak 640 computer/notetaker (includes talking clock, calculator, calendar, phone directory) which can also be used as input device for DOS computers; Type 'n Speak computer/notetaker with standard keyboard.

Disabilities: blindness, low vision

22. BOSSERT Specialties, Inc.

P.O. Box 15441
Phoenix, AZ 85060

Street Address:
The Magnification Center
3620 E. Thomas Road
Suite D 124
Phoenix, AZ 85018

Tel. (800) 776-5885
      (602) 956-6637
Fax (602) 956-1008

Comment: Sells over 600 software and hardware products for a variety of disabilities, primarily for those with low vision. Products include CCTVs (Optelec, Humanware Magnisight, SeeTec) LP-DOS, Zoomtext, Humanware products, speech synthesizers (Echo, Accent, DECtalk). Computer products for IBM and compatibles, Apple II, Macintosh. Also sells Reading Edge machine and magnifiers. Produces a catalog of merchandise sold.

Disabilities: low vision, blindness, hearing, speech, physical

23. Brown & Company, Inc.

P.O. Box 861
Georgetown, MA 01833

Tel. (508) 352-8822 voice and
      fax

Comment: Manufactures and sells the PC Pedal, an alternative keyboard device that allows one-handed operation of the computer keyboard. This external switching device (usually a foot pedal, but can be other type of switch) duplicates the shift, alt, ctrl, and backspace keys. Enhanced software is available for duplicating any key.

Disabilities: physical, mental, carpal tunnel syndrome

24. Carroll Center for the Blind

770 Centre Street
Newton, MA 02158

Tel. (800) 852-3131
      (617) 969-6200
Fax (617) 969-6204

Comment: Carroll Center for the Blind is a school that offers evaluation, assessment, consultation, rehabilitation and computer training. The school will offer on-site training nationwide, provides instruction for teachers for college credit, and conducts an international program and a program for youth during the summer. An educational software directory with a vendor list is available from the school for $10.

Disabilities: low vision, blindness

25. Carroll Touch, Inc.

P.O. Box 1309
Round Rock, TX 78680

Tel. (512) 244-3500
Fax (512) 244-7040

Comment: Manufactures a variety of touch screens for computer monitors. Sells direct. Also sells and customizes kiosks. Inquire about evaluation units available for trial period.

Disabilities: learning, physical

26. Centigram Communications Corp.

91 E. Tasman Drive
San Jose, CA 95134

Tel. (408) 944-0250
Fax (408) 428-3732

Comment: Manufactures Adaptive Information Processing (AIP) software that integrates voice, data, and facsimile by providing access through telephone or PC.

Disabilities: hearing, vision, speech

27. Computer Conversations

6297 Worthington Road SW
Alexandria, OH 43001

Tel. (614) 924-2885
     (614) 263-7574
Fax (614) 924-2221

Comment: Manufactures and sells the Verbette voice synthesizer (Verbette I is internal; Verbette II is external) and sells the Verbal Operating System voice output software.

Disabilities: speech and hearing

28. Computer Furniture Design and Manufacturing Craner Cabinetry

3190 S. 4140 West
West Valley City, UT 84120

Tel. (801) 966-1127

Comment: Manufactures adjustable computer tables for wheelchair access or other physical disabilities. Three designs are available on a made-to-order basis, or they will build to suit. Brochures on existing styles are available.

Disabilities: physical

29. Computer Prompting and Captioning Company

3408 Wisconsin Avenue
Washington, DC 20016

Tel. (800) 977-6678
     (202) 966-0980
     (202) 966-0886 TDD
Fax (202) 966-0981

Comment: Manufactures two software products for open or closed captioning of existing videotapes, CaptionMaker and CaptionMaker Plus (IBM-compatible software). Also sells hardware related to captioning (data recovery decoder and encoder card) and provides captioning services and subtitling services.

Disabilities: hearing, deafness, learning

30. Covox, Inc.

675 Conger Street
Eugene, OR 97402

Tel. (503) 342-1271
Fax (503) 342-1283

Comment: Sells voice recognition products for the IBM PC and compatibles. Products include VoiceMaster, a voice input, speech output device, available as an internal card or external device, and SpeechThing, an output device that converts text to speech. A catalog is available.

Disabilities: learning, physical, low vision

31. Creative Switch Industries
P.O. Box 5256
Des Moines, IA 50306

Tel. (800) 257-4385
(515) 287-5748

Comment: Mail order company that manufactures and sells a variety of ability switches. Products are sold direct and through dealers. Also sells an electrical control unit/AC adapter that converts an electrical appliance to switch use. A free catalog of products is available.

Disabilities: physical, learning

32. Crestwood Company
Communication Aids for
Children and Adults
6625 N. Sidney Place
Milwaukee, WI 53209-3259

Tel. (414) 352-5678

Comment: Mail order company that specializes in communications solutions like talking pictures, communication boards, voice amplifiers, mounting packages and switches, and toys.

Disabilities: physical, hearing, speech, mental

33. Demco, Inc.
P.O. Box 7488
Madison, WI 53707-7488

Tel. (800) 356-1200
Fax (800) 245-1329

Comment: Sells furniture, compliance guidebooks, videotapes, braille signage, page turners and other products.

Disabilities: physical

34. Digital Equipment Corp.
Assistive Technology Access
Center
30 Forbes Road
NRO5/14
Northboro, MA 01532

Tel. (800) 344-4825 for orders
(800) 343-4040 for pre-purchase technical assistance

Comment: Manufactures and sells DECtalk internal voice synthesizer PC option card (Model DTC 07-AA). The Center is also a demonstration site for various products, including speech recognition and voice output products.

Disabilities: low vision, blindness

35. Don Johnston, Inc.

P.O. Box 639
1000 N. Rand Road
Building 115
Wauconda, IL 60084-0639

Tel. (800) 999-4660 US and
Canada
(708) 526-2682 International
Fax (708) 526-4177

Comment: Product developer, manufacturer and reseller, and vendor of products of other manufacturers, Don Johnston sells a wide variety of adaptive software and hardware for Macintosh and Apple II series computers. Products include Ke:nx for Macintosh, Co:Writer word prediction software, Write:OutLoud talking word processor for Macintosh, educational software, keyboard enhancements, moisture guards for keyboards, alternative keyboards and overlay kits, keyguards, switches, mounting systems and battery adapters, and speech synthesizers. Products are available for a 14-day trial. Demonstration copies or instructional videos available on some equipment. Call for details.

Disabilities: physical, developmental, learning

36. Dots-On Enterprises

1901 N. Baylen Street
Pensacola, FL 32501

Tel. (904) 432-0894
Fax (904) 432-0894 (same as above)

Comment: Factory regional representative for Xerox Imaging Systems/Kurzweil Products, Seeing Technologies, and dealer for Artic Technologies, Raised Dot Computing and Blazie Engineering products. Also offers training and consultation.

Disabilities: low vision, blindness, learning

37. Dragon Systems, Inc.

320 Nevada Street
Newton, MA 02160

Tel. (800) 825-5897
(617) 965-5200
Fax (617) 527-0372
(617) 332-9575

Comment: Developer of speech input software for IBM and other DOS environment computers. Dragon Systems is an IBM Authorized Industry Remarketer. Products include DragonDictate, IBM VoiceType.

Disabilities: physical, learning

38. DU-IT Control Systems Group, Inc.

8765 Township Road 513
Shreve, OH 44676-9421

Tel. (216) 567-2001
Fax (216) 567-3925

Comment: Manufactures, sells direct and through selected dealers, alternative input devices. Primary products are LIAISON, a complete computer workstation, keyboard and mouse, for severe mobility impairment (operated by the chin, tongue and/or lips); DEUCE, an environmental control device (can control telephone, TV, hospital bed, stereo, etc.); and ROVER, a specialized, integrated wheelchair control system. Also sells additional accessories.

Disabilities: mobility, physical (specifically high spinal cord injury and advanced muscular dystrophy, individuals without limbs)

39. Duxbury Systems, Inc.
435 King Street
P.O. Box 1504
Littleton, MA 01460

Tel. (508) 486-9766
Fax (508) 486-9712
Compuserve   76150,2046

Comment: Manufactures and sells products for the blind and visually impaired. Product line includes braille translators, braille editors, braille translator for WordPerfect, braille fonts. Also publishes a semi-annual newsletter, and offers consulting and training.

Disabilities: blindness, low vision

40. E R and S Computer Solutions, Inc.
14711 N.E. 29th Place
Suite 218
Bellevue, WA 98007

Tel. (800) 348-8829
     (206) 881-1789
Fax (206) 883-7136

Comment: Sells Pronounce, a speech recognition system for the IBM PC or PS/2 which allows voice input as an alternative to the keyboard.

Disabilities: physical, low vision, blindness

41. Eastern Electronics Corp.
(formerly American Communication Corp.)
180 Roberts Street
East Hartford, CT 06108

Tel. (203) 289-3491
     (203) 528-9821
Fax (203) 289-7639

Comment: Manufactures, sells direct and through dealers TDD LUV I (Display unit only—does not have printer capability). Also sells light signal indicators.

Disabilities: speech, deafness, hearing

42. Echo Speech Corp.
(formerly Street Electronics Corp.)
6460 Via Real
Carpinteria, CA 93013

Tel. (805) 684-4593
Fax (805) 684-6628

Comment: Manufactures and sells speech synthesizers for Apple II, Macintosh and IBM computers.

Disabilities: blindness, low vision

43. Edmark Corporation
P.O. Box 3218
Redmond, WA 98073-3218

Street Address:
6727 185th Avenue, NE
Redmond, WA 98052

Tel. (800) 426-0856
     (206) 556-8400
     (206) 556-8402 TDD
Fax (206) 556-8998

Comment: Publishes and distributes educational software and print material for use in early childhood, remedial and speech education markets. Products include software for IBM, Apple, Macintosh, Tandy computers. Edmark also assembles and distributes the TouchWindow, a touch-sensitive input device that can be mounted on computer monitors. TouchWindow is available for IBM, Macintosh, Apple II, and Amiga computers.

Disabilities: learning, physical, mental, low vision, speech

44. Educational Activities, Inc.

P.O. Box 392
Freeport, NY 11520

Tel. (800) 645-3739
     (516) 223-4666 New York
     only
Fax (516) 623-9282

Comment: Sells the LAPTALK portable talking computer, with voice input and output; runs MS-DOS software. Also sells educational interactive software.

Disabilities: learning, blindness, low vision

45. EKEG Electronics Co. Ltd.

P.O. Box 46199
Station D
Vancouver, British Columbia
Canada
V6J 5G5

Tel. (604) 273-4358
Fax (604) 273-1148

Comment: Manufactures and sells expanded and mini-keyboards for most computers, some learning aids, and a memory speakerphone. They plug into the keyboard socket of the computer (not the serial port) and are "transparent," i.e., no interface card or special software is required. Keyguards are also available. Also manufactures the MACRAT, an expanded keyboard mouse for the Macintosh and Apple IIGs computers, and the BIG BLUE mouse, an expanded keyboard mouse for the IBM.

Disabilities: physical

46. Enabling Technologies Company

3102 S. E. Jay Street
Stuart, FL 34997

Tel. (800) 777-3687
     (407) 283-4817
Fax (407) 220-2920

Comment: Manufactures braille printers and a telephone communication device (INFOTOUCH) for deaf/blind braille readers. Sells products direct and through branches in Kansas, Atlanta, and Washington, D.C. It also markets software products for IBM, Apple and Macintosh computers, including braille translation software and software used to produce braille graphics.

Disabilities: deafness, blindness

47. EVAS Company

(Electronic Visual Aid Specialists)
57C Shore Road
Westerly, RI 02891

Tel. (800) 872-3827
     (401) 596-3155
Fax (401) 596-3979

Comment: EVAS manufactures and distributes a wide range of adaptive aids for the visually impaired and physically challenged, including speech synthesizers, screen readers, large print software, CCTVs, refreshable braille displays, braille printers, OCR reading systems, specialized keyboards, ability switches and voice recognition system and TDD products.

Disabilities: low vision, blindness, physical, speech, learning

48. Exceptional Computing
450 N.W. 58th Street
Gainesville, FL 32607

Tel. (904) 331-8847
Fax (904) 331-4164
AppleLink   IT.Sales

Comment: Sells software and hardware for IBM, Apple II, and Macintosh computers for a variety of disabilities. Much of the software is speech and language software targeted for the profoundly disabled. Hardware products include alternative keyboards, speech synthesizers, Ke:nx and various switches. Also manufactures an adaptive musical keyboard. Provides technical support. A complete catalog of products is available.

Disabilities: physical, low vision, blindness, developmental

49. Exceptional Teaching Aids
20102 Woodbine Avenue
Castro Valley, CA 94546

Tel. (800) 549-6999
     (510) 582-4859
Fax (510) 582-5911

Comment: Sells educational products and supplies for special needs students with specific emphasis on students with visual impairments. Products include braille reading programs and talking software for Apple and IBM computers. A free catalog of products is available.

Disabilities: low vision, learning

50. Extensions for Independence
555 Saturn Blvd.
San Diego, CA 92154

Tel. (619) 423-7709
Fax (619) 423-1748

Comment: Manufactures and sells a wide variety of special devices for physical disabilities with special emphasis on adaptation for working in an office environment. Products include specially designed adjustable desks, mouthsticks, keylocks for computers and other hardware and equipment. A free catalog is available.

Disabilities: physical

51. EZ Reader
3920 Central Avenue
St. Petersburg, FL 33711-1238

Tel. (800) 275-7232

Comment: Markets the EZ-Reader portable handheld video magnification device; connects to a television or monitor to enlarge image on screen.

Disabilities: low vision

52. Florida New Concepts, Inc.
P.O. Box 261
Port Richey, FL 34673-0261

Tel. (800) 456-7097
     (813) 842-3231
Fax (813) 845-7544

Comment: Manufactures and distributes Compu-Lenz, a screen magnifier for computers and Beamscope, a magnifier for television sets.

Disabilities: low vision

53. Fred Sammons, Inc.

145 Tower Drive
Burr Ridge, IL 60521

Address for orders:
P.O. Box 32
Brookfield, IL 60513

Tel. (800) 323-5547
    (708) 325-1700
Fax (800) 547-4333

Comment: Sells a wide variety of self-help and physical therapy products. A free catalog of over 2,000 products is available. Products include door knob handles, ramps, color-coded switches, various computer accessories, mouthsticks, head pointers, speech software, and learning software.

Disabilities: all categories

54. Gaylord Bros.

Products for Library Services to
    the Disabled
Box 4901
Syracuse, NY 13221-4901

Tel. (800) 448-6160 ordering
    (800) 634-6307 customer
    service
Fax (800) 272-3412

Comment: A wide variety of furniture and products to aid patrons with disabilities, including special carrels, desks, and shelving. Products include page turners, tactile maps, screen enlargers, hearing systems, and braille characters.

Disabilities: all categories

55. GW Micro, Inc.

310 Racquet Drive
Fort Wayne, IN 46825

Tel. (219) 483-3625
Fax (219) 484-2510
BBS (219) 484-0210

Comment: Provides computer-based speech products for the visually impaired, including IBM and Apple software, speech synthesizers, talking desktop computer systems and talking laptop computers. Also sells Dragon Dictate, IBM VoiceType, Arkenstone readers and IBM software for learning disabled.

Disabilities: low vision, blindness, learning

56. Handykey Corporation

141 Mount Sinai Avenue
Mount Sinai, NY 11766

Tel. (800) 638-2352
    (516) 474-4405
Fax (516) 474-3760

Comment: Manufactures and sells an alternative keyboard, the Twiddler, a pocket-sized, full-function keyboard and mouse pointer that can be used by one hand and does not require a desk. It can be used in place of a standard keyboard, or used with an existing keyboard. It is used with an IBM or IBM-compatible computer.

Disabilities: physical, repetitive stress injury or carpal tunnel syndrome

57. Harris Communications
6541 City West Parkway
Eden Prairie, MN 55344-3248

Tel. (800) 825-6758
      (612) 946-0921
      (800) 825-9187 TDD
      (612) 946-0922 TDD
Fax (612) 946-0924

Comment: Distributor for products for hearing impaired and deaf. Sells Ultratec TDD; National Captioning Institute's closed captioned decoders; Sonic Alert signalling device; various other assistive listening devices, including alarm clocks, books, and videotapes about deaf culture and sign language.

Disabilities: hearing, deafness

58. Health Care Keyboard Company
N82 W15340
Appleton Avenue
Menomonee Falls, WI 53051

Tel. (414) 253-6333
Fax (414) 253-6330

Comment: Manufactures the Comfort Keyboard System, an alternative keyboard with three separate sections for left hand, right hand, and a numeric keypad. The sections can be adjusted to a variety of positions to meet the needs of the user.

Disabilities: physical

59. Henter-Joyce, Inc.
2100 62nd Avenue
St. Petersburg, FL 33706

Tel. (800) 336-5658 US only
      (813) 576-5658

Fax (813) 577-0099
BBS (813) 579-0099

Comment: Develops and implements products for the blind and visually impaired computer user. Products include JAWS screen reading software, Form-Mate, DEC-talk speech synthesizer. Also sells products of other developers, including braille printers, screen enlarging software and speech synthesizers. Products are for IBM and compatible computers. Also sells Word-Scholar software for learning disabled.

Disabilities: low vision, blindness, learning

60. The Highsmith Co., Inc.
W5527 Highway 106
P.O. Box 800
Fort Atkinson, WI 53538-0800

Tel. (800) 558-2110

Comment: Produces a specialty catalog for ADA compliance products.

Disabilities: all categories

61. Hooleon Corporation
260 Justin Drive
Cottonwood, AZ 86326

Tel. (800) 937-1337
      (602) 634-7515
Fax (602) 634-4620

Comment: Manufactures, sells direct and through distributors, keyboard enhancements for IBM, Apple and Macintosh keyboards. Products include keycaps, keyboard protectors, left-handed keyboards, overlays, braille overlays, color-coded label kit, large print letters. Hooleon will also do custom imprinting of keyboards. A catalog of products is available.

Disabilities: low vision, learning, physical

62. Howe Press of Perkins School for the Blind

175 N. Beacon Street
Watertown, MA 02172

Tel. (617) 924-3490
Fax (617) 926-2027

Comment: Manufactures and sells the Perkins Brailler. Also sells braille paper, styluses and brailling slates. A catalog of products is available.

Disabilities: blindness

63. Howtek, Inc.

21 Park Avenue
Hudson, NH 03051

Tel. (603) 882-5200
Fax (603) 880-3843

Comment: Manufactures a variety of color scanners.

Disabilities: low vision

64. HumanWare, Inc.

6245 King Road
Loomis, CA 95650

Tel. (800) 722-3393
     (916) 652-7253
Fax (916) 652-7296

Comment: Vendor of software and hardware for the visually impaired. Products include speech synthesizers, MasterTouch touch tablet for reading computer screen, screen reading software, screen enlarging software, CCTVs, braille printers/embossers, braille-to-print and print-to-braille machines, and refreshable braille display; also SoundProof, software for learning disabled for IBM computers.

Disabilities: low vision, blindness, learning, dyslexia

65. IBM Independence Series Information Center

Tel. (800) 426-4832 for product
     information
TDD (800) 426-4833

Comment: The above automated attendant telephone service provides recorded messages on how to receive information on the following IBM Independence Series products: Screen Reader; Access DOS; Phone Communicator; Keyguards; VoiceType; Speech/Viewer; THINKable.

Disabilities: all categories

66. ILA, Inc.

(Independent Living Aids)
27 East Mall
Plainview, NY 11803

Tel. (800) 537-2118
     (516) 752-8080
Fax (516) 752-3135

Comment: Mail order company sells products for the visually impaired. Computer-related items include Compu-Lenz, computer keyboard wrist support, anti-glare filters. Also sell braille items.

Disabilities: low vision, blindness

Index Braille Printer Co.

See 12, APR Computer Technology

67. Infogrip, Inc.
1145 Eugenia Place
Suite 201
Carpinteria, CA 93013

Tel. (800) 397-0921
     (805) 566-1049
Fax (805) 566-1079

Comment: Manufactures and distributes the BAT Personal keyboard. Ergonomically designed, it allows input of all keyboard commands with seven keys (one hand). Exclusive ChordEasy software (included) adds power of Wordchords abbreviations and macros. Available in both left- and right-handed models, the BAT keyboard attaches to the keyboard port and can be used singly, in pairs, and with a traditional keyboard.

Disabilities: learning

68. Institute on Applied Technology
Children's Hospital, Fegan Plaza
300 Longwood Avenue
Boston, MA 02115

Tel. (617) 735-6998
Fax (617) 735-6882

Comment: A research and development group that designs and sells hardware and software for IBM or Macintosh Computers. Products include the MultiVoice voice synthesizer; WriteAway word processing communication software with a variety of adaptive features; and MultiPhone, a telephone that can be controlled by a dedicated communication device or computer.

Disabilities: learning, mental, physical, low vision, blindness, speech

69. Intelligent Information Technologies
Station A, Box 5002
Champaign, IL 61825

Street address:
123 W. Main Street
Suite 220
Urbana, IL 61801

Tel. (217) 337-7058
Fax (217) 337-6928

Comment: Developed and sells a brailling software called ED-IT for Windows for IBM computers. A former product, ED-IT for Apple II computers, is available free from the National Braille Association.

Disabilities: blindness

70. IntelliTools, Inc.
(formerly Unicorn Engineering, Inc.)
5221 Central Avenue
Suite 205
Richmond, CA 94804

Tel. (800) 899-6687 USA only
     (510) 528-0670
Fax (510) 528-2225

Comment: Manufactures, sells direct and through distributors, alternative keyboards for Apple and with interfaces for IBM, Macintosh, Tandy and other MS-DOS computers; can also be used with portable communication aids. IntelliTools publishes a free compatibility list. Also sells software, keyguards, cables, a variety of overlay packages, and a slant board.

Disabilities: learning, physical

71. In Touch Systems

11 Westview Road
Spring Valley, NY 10977

Tel. (800) 332-MAGIC
(914) 354-7431

Comment: Manufactures and sells the Magic Wand keyboard, a miniature, full-function computer keyboard, with built-in mouse, designed for individuals with limited or no hand/arm movement. The keyboard works with a handheld wand or mouthstick, has a standard layout, and works with IBM or Apple computers.

Disabilities: physical

72. Itac Systems, Inc.

3113 Benton Street
Garland, TX 75042

Tel. (800) 533-4822
(214) 494-3073
Fax (214) 494-4159

Comment: Manufactures and sells through dealers the Mouse-Trak trackball mouse.

Disabilities: physical, carpal tunnel syndrome

73. J. A. Preston Corp.

P.O. Box 89
Jackson, MI 49204

Tel. (800) 631-7277 customer service
(517) 787-1600 switchboard
(800) 788-2267 switchboard
Fax (517) 789-3299
(800) 245-3765

Comment: Manufactures and sells physical therapy products for rehabilitation and special education. Sells over 1,500 products, including walkers, wheelchair accessories, mats, pulleys, parallel bars, whirlpools, and carry seats. A free catalog is available.

Disabilities: physical, mental, learning

74. Kansys, Inc.

P.O. Box 1070
Lawrence, KS 66044-8070

Tel. (800) 279-4880
(913) 843-0351

Comment: Develops computer products and provides computer-based services for the blind. Sells TurboBraille, a grade II braille translator, and PROVOX screen review program. PROVOX will support a variety of speech synthesizers.

Disabilities: low vision, blindness

75. Key Tronic Corp.

P.O. Box 14687
Spokane, WA 99214

Tel. (800) 262-6006 for technical support and sales only
(509) 928-8000
Fax (509) 927-5224 sales
(509) 927-5248

Comment: Manufactures and sells, through dealers, alternative input devices, specifically alternative keyboards, programmable keyboards, trackball keyboards, wrist pads.

Disabilities: physical

76. Kinetic Designs, Inc.
14231 Anateyka Lane SE
Olalla, WA 98359

Tel. (206) 857-7943
Fax (206) 857-2640

Comment. Produces software for alternative uses of traditional keyboard. Products are Filch, a keyboard filter program that allows one-handed or mouthstick operation and MorseK which enables the computer to accept morse code input.

Disabilities: physical

77. K R I Communications, Inc.
(Krown Research, Inc.)
3303 Harbor Blvd., Suite D7
Costa Mesa, CA 92626

Tel. (800) 833-4968
(714) 540-7777
Fax (714) 540-7747

Comment: Manufactures and sells a full line of TDDs (telecommunication devices for the deaf)

Disabilities: deafness, hearing

Krown Research, Inc.
See 77, K R I Communications, Inc.

78. Kurzweil Applied Intelligence, Inc.
411 Waverley Oaks Road
Waltham, MA 02154

Tel. (800) 238-6423
(617) 893-5151
Fax (617) 893-6525

Comment: Manufactures and sells the Kurzweil Voice product, a voice-activated personal computing system for use with IBM computers and IBM compatibles.

Disabilities: physical, learning

79. LC Technologies, Inc.
9455 Silver King Court
Fairfax, VA 22031

Tel. (800) 733-5284
(703) 385-7133
Fax (703) 385-7137

Comment: Manufactures and sells the Eyegaze computer system, a vision controlled system providing keyboard emulation, environmental control, and speech output. Provides installation, training, and support for the system.

Disabilities: mobility, hearing

80. LS & S Group, Inc.
P.O. Box 673
Northbrook, IL 60065

Tel. (800) 468-4789
(708) 498-9777
Fax (708) 498-1482

Comment: LS & S distributes a wide variety of adaptive products, including software, hardware, standalone adaptive aids, switches, input and output devices, CCTV, voice synthesizers, etc. A comprehensive catalog is available.

Disabilities: low vision, blindness, mobility, physical

81. Luminaud, Inc.
8688 Tyler Blvd.
Mentor, OH 44060

Tel. (216) 255-9082
Fax (216) 255-2250

Comment: Manufactures the Cooper Rand artificial larynx; also sells supplies for laryngectomees, including switches for the mobility impaired.

Disabilities: speech, physical

82. Madenta Communications, Inc.
9411A 20th Avenue
Edmonton, Alberta
Canada
T6N 1E5

Tel. (800) 661-8406 US and
Canada
(403) 450-8926
Fax (403) 988-6128

Comment: Manufactures, sells direct and through distributors, DOORS adapted access and word prediction software for the Macintosh computer; sells software, which allows voice control with word prediction. Also manufactures and sells PROXi, an environmental control unit which allows for voice environmental control.

Disabilities: physical, speech

83. MAXI AIDS
P.O. Box 3209
Farmingdale, NY 11735

Street address:
42 Executive Blvd.
Farmingdale, NY 11735

Tel. (800) 522-6294 for orders
(516) 752-0521

Fax (516) 752-0689 24 hours a
day

Comment: Mail order company which sells a wide variety of adaptive aids and devices for all disability categories; especially strong in aids for the blind and visually impaired. Complete catalog available.

Disabilities: all categories

84. MacIntyre Computer Systems Division
22809 Shagbark Road
Birmingham, MI 48025

Tel. (313) 645-5090
Fax (313) 645-6042

Comment: Manufactures the LipStick, an alternative input device that replaces a mouse and is mouth-controlled; also sells a software product, WordWriter, an on-screen keyboard with a built-in prediction dictionary.

Disabilities: physical, learning

85. Microflip, Inc.
11211 Petworth Lane
Glenn Dale, MD 20769

Tel. (301) 262-6020 voice and
TDD
Fax (301) 262-4978

Comment: Sells an internal modem for the PC which converts the PC or PS/2 to a TDD. Includes answering machine capability.

Disabilities: hearing, deafness

86. Microspeed, Inc.
5005 Brandin Court
Freemont, CA 94538-3140

Tel. (800) 232-7888
     (510) 490-1403
Fax (510) 490-1665

Comment: Designs, manufactures and sells (direct and through dealers) alternative input devices, specifically trackball devices; the PC TRAC for IBM and MacTRAC for Macintosh. Also sells standard keyboards and mice.

Disabilities: physical, carpal tunnel syndrome, hand/eye coordination problems

87. Microsystems Software Inc.
600 Worcester Road
Framingham, MA 01701-5342

Tel. (800) 828-2600
     (508) 879-9000
Fax (508) 626-8515

Comment: Developer of software for IBM and compatible PCs for individuals requiring adapted access, augmentative communication, low vision and environmental control enhancements.

Disabilities: physical, low vision

88. MicroTouch Systems, Inc.
300 Griffin Park
Methuen, MA 01844-9867

Tel. (800) UNMOUSE
     (508) 659-9000
Fax (508) 659-9100

Comment: Manufactures touch screens for computers.

Disabilities: physical, learning

89. Mons International
P.O. Box 84162
Atlanta, GA 30341

Street Address:
6595 Roswell Road #224
Atlanta, GA 30328

Tel. (404) 551-8455
     (800) 541-7903

Comment: Mail order products for the blind and visually impaired including lighting, colored filters, occluders, magnifiers, and telescopes.

Disabilities: low vision, blindness

MTI, Inc.
See 40, E R & S Computer Solutions, Inc.

90. NanoPac, Inc.
4833 S. Sheridan Road
Suite 402
Tulsa, OK 74145-5718

Tel. (918) 665-0329
Fax (918) 665-0361

Comment: Sells the Cintex communication aid software for IBM computers. Cintex has word processing and environmental control capabilities. Also sells Cintex II, a voice-activated environmental control system; includes control of telephone, appliances, television, stereo, etc. Also dealer for IBM ThinkAble, SpeechViewer, Dragon Dictate, Screen Reader, IBM VoiceType.

Disabilities: physical, motor

Nassau Applied Technology Research Center
See 125, United Cerebral Palsy of Nassau County

91. National Captioning Institute

5203 Leesburg Pike
Suite 1500
Falls Church, VA 22041

Tel. (800) 533-9673
     (703) 998-2400
Fax (703) 998-2458

Comment: Manufacturer only. Sells products through distributors, no direct sales. Product is AudioLink Personal Listening System, a wireless listening device that amplifies sound from television (PLS-100), or in specially equipped public facilities (PLS-110). A listing of AudioLink-compatible public facilities is available from NCI. Also markets two models of closed caption decoders, the Telecaption 4000 and the Telecaption VR-100.

Disabilities: hearing, deafness, learning

92. National Institute for Rehabilitation Engineering

P.O. Box T
Hewitt, NJ 07421

Tel. (201) 853-6585

Comment: A consulting service, NIRE will advise individuals of products available to meet their needs, acquire and customize equipment, and produce a training video for its use.

Disabilities: all categories

93. Nationwide Flashing Signal Systems, Inc.

8120 Fenton Street
Silver Spring, MD 20910

Tel. (301) 589-6671
     (301) 589-6670 TTY
Fax (301) 589-5153

Comment: Sells assistive listening devices for the deaf and hearing impaired, TTYs, decoders. Free catalog available.

Disabilities: hearing, deafness

94. New DEST Corp.

4180 Business Center Drive
Fremont, CA 94538

Tel. (510) 249-0330
Fax (510) 249-0344

Comment: Manufactures and sells the DEST computer optical scanners (flatbed and page fed) which do OCR and graphics.

Disabilities: low vision

95. Optelec U.S.A., Inc.

P.O. Box 729
6 Lyberty Way
Westford, MA 01886

Tel. (800) 828-1056
     (508) 392-0707
Fax (508) 692-6073

Comment: Manufactures and sells directly, and through dealers, low vision reading equipment for the visually impaired. Products include the Twenty/20 CCTV, Twenty/20 Plus, Jr. Spectrum, Bright Eye, LP-DOS (Large print DOS). Representatives will rent equipment out for trial.

Disabilities: low vision, hearing, deafness, mobility, learning, speech

96. Personal Data Systems
100 W. Rincon Avenue
Suite 103
Campbell, CA 95003

Tel. (408) 866-1126
Fax (408) 866-1128

Comment: Manufactures and sells direct, and through dealers, Audapter external speech system (speech synthesizer) and integrates personal information systems, including CD-ROMs, braille translators, braille embossers.

Disabilities: visual, learning, speech, motor

97. Phone TTY, Inc.
202 Lexington Avenue
Hackensack, NJ 07601

Tel. (201) 489-7889 Voice
(201) 489-7890 TDD
Fax (201) 489-7891

Comment: Sells TTYs, signallers, closed caption decoders, external modems for IBM-compatible computers. A complete catalog is available without charge.

Disabilities: hearing, deafness

98. Phonic Ear, Inc.
3880 Cypress Drive
Petaluma, CA 94954-7600

Tel. (800) 227-0735
(707) 769-1110
(707) 769-1110 TDD
Fax (707) 769-9624

Comment: Manufactures, sells direct and through distributors, Free Field sound system, the Easy Listener Personal FM amplification system, and the Vois 160 communication aid with P.A.L.L.S. or VoisShapes software.

Disabilities: hearing, learning, attention deficit, speech

99. Pointer Systems, Inc.
1 Mill Street
Burlington, VT 05401-1529

Tel. (802) 658-3260
Fax (802) 658-3714

Comment: Manufactures and sells two products for the disability market, HeadMouse, a mouse operated by head movement. Based on infrared optical technology the cordless optical head pointer replaces the mouse for Windows 3.1. Also sells the Hawkeye, another alternative to the mouse. Hawkeye is a miniature pointing device similar to a penlight.

Disabilities: mobility, learning, speech

100. Polytel Computer Products Corp.
1287 Hammerwood Avenue
Sunnyvale, CA 94089

Tel. (800) 245-6655
(408) 745-1540
Fax (408) 745-6340

Comment: Manufactures and sells the Keyport alternative keyboard for IBM computers.

Disabilities: mobility, learning

101. Potomac Technology, Inc.
1 Church Street
Suite 402
Rockville, MD 20850

Tel. (800) 433-2838 voice or TDD
(301) 762-4005 voice
(301) 762-0851 TDD
(301) 762-1892

Comment: Sells the Ultratec line of TDDs and other assistive listening devices. A full catalog is available free upon request.

Disabilities: hearing, deafness

102. Prentke Romich Company
1022 Heyl Road
Wooster, OH 44691

Tel. (800) 262-1984
(216) 262-1984
Fax (216) 263-4829
(800) 262-1990 toll-free line for 24-hour service only

Canada:
(800) 253-1984 sales
(800) 253-1989 24-hour service

International:
(216) 262-8031 24-hour service

Regional Consultant:
(800) 848-8008

Comment: Manufactures and markets augmentative communication devices. Products include alternative input devices, keyboard enhancements, keyguards, disk guides, wheelchair mounting kits, switches, sensors. Computer products are available for both IBM and Macintosh computers.

Prentke Romich also offers a rental program to try out its devices, seminars on its various products, and provides a network of regional consultants nationwide who assist in selection of devices and training.

Disabilities: physical

103. Productivity Software International, Inc.
211 E. 43rd Street
New York, NY 10017

Tel. (212) 818-1144
Fax (212) 818-1197

Comment: Produces PRD+ (Productivity Plus), MS-DOS, command driven software that enables the user to type abbreviations instead of entire words on the keyboard (keyboard macro). Also has a sticky key function. PRD+ is available in 32 different pre-programmed packages as well as the basic edition and works together with existing word processing, database or spreadsheet software.

Disabilities: physical, learning, dyslexia, low vision, blindness

104. ProHance Technologies, Inc.
1172-D Asper Avenue
Sunnyvale, CA 94086

Tel. (408) 246-4390
Fax (408) 246-8243

Comment: Manufactures programmable, multi-button mice which replace the keyboard and/or mouse for computer input. Products include the PowerTrack trackball mouse with 40 programmable buttons. Sells direct and also through selected dealers.

Disabilities: physical

105. Raised-Dot Computing, Inc.
408 S. Baldwin Street
Madison, WI 53703

Tel. (800) 347-9594
(608) 257-9595
Fax (608) 241-2498

Comment: Produces, sells direct and through distributors, word processing and braille translation software for IBM PC and Apple II computers. Premier product is Megadots, a combination word processing and braille translation program with optional spellchecker. Megadots will correct errors made by optical character recognition systems. Also sells Talk-to-Me audiotape tutorials for Wordperfect, Lotus 1-2-3, DBase and ProComm.

Disabilities: low vision, blindness

106. Reading Access Products
1739 Hickory Shores Road
Gulf Breeze, FL 32561

Tel. (904) 934-4804 voice or fax

Comment: Southeastern factory representative for Xerox Imaging Systems/Kurzweil line of reading machines, and reseller for Artic Technologies products, BVDK and Focus.

Disabilities: low vision, learning

107. Reflection Technology, Inc.
230 Second Avenue
Waltham, MA 02154

Tel. (617) 890-5905
Fax (617) 890-5918

Comment: Manufactures and sells the Private Eye, a miniature virtual display device (1"x1"x3") that displays the same amount of information shown on a desk top computer monitor; primarily sold to companies who will incorporate it into an existing system (e.g., Optelec's Bright Eye). It can be used with a wheelchair mounting system or headset.

Disabilities: low vision, learning, hearing, mobility

108. Roudley Associates, Inc.
P.O. Box 608
Owings Mills, MD 21117

Tel. (410) 363-7049
(800) 333-7049

Comment: Manufactures and sells software for IBM PC clones. Also manufactures NFB-TRANS, which translates text to braille.

Disabilities: blindness

109. Scott Instruments Corp.
1111 Willow Springs Drive
Denton, TX 76205

Tel. (817) 387-9514
Fax (817) 566-3174

Comment: Research and development corporation that develops speech recognition and voice processing hardware and software. Products include Sir Model 20, ThruTalk and Coretech.

Disabilities: physical

110. Seeing Technologies, Inc.

7074 Brooklyn Blvd.
Minneapolis, MN 55429

Tel. (800) 462-3738
     (612) 560-8080
Fax (612) 560-0663

Comment: Manufactures and sells direct and through regional representatives CCTVs for low vision. Also sells MAGIC, large print computer software for IBMs and compatibles.

Disabilities: low vision

111. Sentient Systems Technology, Inc.

2100 Wharton Street
Pittsburgh, PA 15203

Tel. (800) 344-1778
     (412) 381-4883
Fax (412) 381-5241

Comment: Manufacturer and reseller of augmentative communicative devices. Products include DynaVox and DigiVox.

Disabilities: speech, physical, mental, low vision, blindness

112. Sight Source, Inc.

P.O. Box 14577
Bradenton, FL 34280

Tel. (800) 648-2266

Comment: Manufacturer of Opteq Vision Systems CCTVs including i-Trak, a new mini handheld reader which can be used with any TV. Also a free national mail-order catalog, Carolyn's, which features over 400 items for visually impaired persons, including Eye Quest CCTVs, talking products, software, synthesizers, handheld magnifiers, and many more products.

Disabilities: low vision, blindness

113. Softcraft, Inc.

16 N. Carroll Street
Suite 220
Madison, WI 53703

Tel. (800) 351-0500
     (608) 257-3300
Fax (608) 257-6733

Comment: Software developer; produces large print software for the IBM PC or compatible and includes a variety of fonts and styles.

Disabilities: low vision

Street Electronics Corp.

See 42, Echo Speech Corp.

114. Syntha-voice Computers, Inc.

1925 Pine Avenue
Suite 9009
Niagara Falls, NY 14301

800 Queenston Road
Suite 304
Stoney Creek, Ontario
Canada
L8G 1A7

Tel. (800) 263-4540 for orders and customer support only
     (905) 662-0565
Fax (905) 662-0568
BBS (905) 662-0569

Comment: Research and development company that produces and sells software for IBM computers; including speech output and large print; specializes in accessing Microsoft Windows, DOS and network environments. Also sells VOCATE, a software program for individuals with learning disabilities.

Disabilities: low vision, blindness, learning, speech, dyslexia

115. Tapeswitch Corp.

100 Schmitt Blvd.
Farmingdale, NY 11735

Tel. (800) 234-TAPE
(516) 694-6312
Fax (516) 694-6304

Comment: Manufactures electric sensing switches, sensing edges, and sensing mats, in various pressure sensitivities. A free catalog of products is available.

Disabilities: motor, physical

116. TASH, Inc.

(Technical Aids & Systems for the Handicapped, Inc.)
91 Station Street
Unit 1
Ajax, Ontario
Canada
L1S 3H2

Tel. (905) 686-4129
Fax (905) 686-6895

Comment: Sells adaptive keyboards, keyguards, Next Page page turner, switches, PC and Mac mini keyboards, mouse emulators, disk guides, and environmental controls. A free catalog is available.

Disabilities: physical, learning

117. Technology for Language and Learning, Inc.

P.O. Box 327
East Rockaway, NY 11518-0327

Tel. (516) 625-4550
Fax (516) 621-3321

Comment: Technology for Language and Learning is a nonprofit organization and has a collection of over 350 special education public domain volumes for the Apple II and Macintosh LC with a IIe Emulation Board. There are programs for the keyboard, joystick, the PowerPad, Touch Window, Echo, and for single switch use. TLL has programs that are appropriate to use with individuals who have language disorders, aphasia, learning problems, visual impairments, hearing impairments, and physical disabilities. A complete catalog with detailed descriptions of each program is available for $10.

Disabilities: learning, mental

118. Telesensory Corp.

455 N. Bernardo Avenue
Mountain View, CA 96043

Tel. (800) 227-8418 customer
support
(415) 960-0920
Fax (415) 969-9064
(800) 537-3961 for technical
support only
Telex 278838 TSI UR

Comment: Manufactures, sells direct and through distributors, products for the blind and visually impaired. Product line includes CCTVs, computer magnification systems, speech output software and speech synthesizers, braille printers, braille translators, braille output display, a handheld braille computer, refreshable braille display, and a braille graphic image producer. Also publishes a free monthly newsletter, *Focus on Technology.*

Disabilities: low vision, blindness, learning

119. Tiger Communication System, Inc.
155 E. Broad Street
Suite 325
Rochester, NY 14604

Tel. (800) 724-7301
(716) 454-5134

Comment: Sells a picture communication system with option of one of three electronic voice output keyboards. The keyboards offer single word output, single sentence output, or single sentence output with up to 26 stored sentences. Keyboards can also be used separately. A videotape and print material of the product are available.

Disabilities: speech, learning, head injuries, visual

120. Touch Turner Company
443 View Ridge Drive
Everett, WA 98203

Tel. (206) 252-1541
Fax (206) 259-4390

Comment: Manufactures and sells the Touch Turner page turner.

Disabilities: physical

121. Toys for Special Children
385 Warburton Avenue
Hastings-on-Hudson, NY 10706

Tel. (800) 832-8697
(914) 478-0960
Fax (914) 478-7030

Comment: Sells a variety of adaptive aids for Apple and IBM computers, including keyboard covers and a wide variety of switches, adapters and environmental control devices, and mounting systems. A complete catalog is available.

Disabilities: learning, mobility, physical

122. Trace Research and Development Center
Room S-151 Waisman Center
University of Wisconsin
1500 Highland Avenue
Madison, WI 53705-2280

Tel. (608) 262-6966
(608) 263-5408 TDD

Comment: A multidisciplinary research and resource center on technology and human disability, Trace Center provides assistance to individuals, businesses, and educational institutions. A free catalog of information and products sold is available.

Disabilities: all categories

123. Typewriting Institute for the Handicapped
3102 W. Augusta Avenue
Phoenix, AZ 85051

Tel. (602) 939-5344
Fax (602) 870-9371

Comment: Primary product is a typewriter or IBM computer keyboard for one-hand operation. Also sells a large print typewriter.

Disabilities: physical

124. Ultratec, Inc.
450 Science Drive
Madison, WI 53711

Tel. (800) 482-2424
(608) 238-5400 voice and
TDD
Fax (608) 238-3008

Comment: Manufactures and sells the Ultratec line of TDDs.

Disabilities: hearing, deafness

Unicorn Engineering, Inc.
See 70, IntelliTools, Inc.

125. United Cerebral Palsy of Nassau County
Nassau Applied Technology
Resource Center
380 Washington Avenue
Roosevelt, NY 11575

Tel. (516) 378-2000, ext. 263
(Rehabilitation Technology
Dept.)
Fax (516) 378-0357

Comment: Manufactures mobility devices, seating devices, switches and communication devices for a variety of disabilities. Will also customize devices according to an individual's need. A full catalog is available.

Disabilities: all categories

126. University Copy Services, Inc.
2405 Bond Street
University Park, IL 60466

Tel. (800) 762-2736
(708) 534-1502
Fax (708) 534-8460

Comment: Exclusive distributor for the Selectec BookMaster copier, a copying machine with a foot pedal for hands-free operation, and a topless feature with retina shield. The copier also has a front slant feature for copying pages from a book. Braille instructions available.

Disabilities: physical

127. Verbex
1090 King Georges Post Road
Bldg. 107
Edison, NJ 08837

Tel. (800) ASK VRBX

Comment: Sells one key product: Listen for Windows, a continuous speech recognition system for Windows.

Disabilities: low vision, blindness, mental

128. VIS-AIDS, Inc.
P.O. Box 180026
102-09 Jamaica Avenue
Richmond Hills, NY 11418

Tel. (800) 346-9579
(718) 847-4734
Fax (718) 441-2550

Comment: Mail order company with items for the blind and visually impaired. Products include CompuLenz and non-computer-related adaptive aids, such as talking clocks, talking calculators, talking watches, canes, low vision clocks, and magnifiers.

Disabilities: low vision, blindness

129. Vision Outreach, Inc.
2100 Constitution Blvd.
Sarasota, FL 34231

Tel. (800) 284-2020
     (813) 346-3937
Fax (813) 921-7105

Comment: Sells CCTVs and magnifiers.

Disabilities: low vision

130. Voice Connection
17835 Skypark Circle
Suite C
Irvine, CA 92714

Tel. (714) 261-2366
Fax (714) 261-8563

Comment: Manufactures voice recognition products for IBM and compatible computers.

Disabilities: speech, physical, blindness

131. Votan, a Division of MOSCOM Corp.
6920 Koll Center Parkway #214
Pleasanton, CA 94566

Tel. (800) 877-4756
     (510) 426-5600
Fax (510) 426-6767

Comment: MOSCOM supplies high performance PC-based voice processing, voice recognition, and voice authentication products. One of these products, the VPC2100, is a single channel recognition card for use in home and office environments where keyboard access is not possible. This IBM-PC compatible voice board controls all computer and telephone functions through use of simple spoken commands. MOSCOM, through its Votan Division, services the handicapped market primarily through two of its VARs, HTI (303-695-0609) and Equal Access (313-694-3755), who have created complete handicapped system products based on Votan's VoiceKey TSR program. Versions of VoiceKey are available for both DOS and Windows 3.1.

Disabilities: low vision, blindness

132. Walker Equipment Corporation
Highway 151 South
Ringgold, GA 30736

Tel. (800) 426-3738
     (706) 935-2600
Fax (706) 935-4603

Comment: Sells amplified handsets for telephones.

Disabilities: hearing

133. WesTest Engineering Corporation
1470 N. Main Street
Bountiful, UT 84010

Tel. (801) 298-7100
Fax (801) 292-7379

Comment: Manufactures and sells DARCI TOO, a universal input device (keyboard and mouse emulator) used to operate a personal computer; it can be controlled by switches, joysticks, video game controllers, a matrix keyboard or communication aids. A videotape of DARCI TOO is available.

Disabilities: physical

134. Words+, Inc.
P.O. Box 1229
Lancaster, CA 93584

Street address:
40015 Sierra Highway
Palmdale, CA 93550

Tel. (800) 869-8521 USA and
Canada
(805) 949-8331 sales or
product information

Comment: Produces software for augmentative communication systems and sells accompanying hardware (e.g., voice synthesizers, lap-top computer). Software products include keyboard enhancers, keyboard macros, speech output, all products for IBM computers. Also sells Simplicity wheelchair mount and U-control environmental control transmitter.

Disabilities: low vision, hearing, deafness, mobility, learning, speech

135. Xerox Imaging Systems, Inc.
9 Centenniao Drive
Peabody, MA 01960

Tel. (800) 248-6550 orders and
technical support
(800) 421-7323 customer
service and sales
(508) 977-2000
Fax (508) 977-2148 orders

Comment: Markets the Kurzweil reading machines that convert text to speech, Reading AdvantEdge and BookWise software.

Disabilities: low vision, learning, print

136. ZYGO Industries, Inc.
P.O. Box 1008
Portland, OR 97207-1008

Tel. (800) 234-6006
(503) 684-6006
Fax (503) 684-6011

Comment: Manufactures, sells direct and through authorized dealers, communication systems for speech impaired; also offers computer access products for IBM-compatible computers, including environmental control products, page turners, scanning input devices, alternative keyboards, switches and mounting systems. Also sells door openers and adaptive elevator control systems. A catalog of products is available.

Disabilities: low vision, blindness, hearing, deafness, mobility, learning, speech, physical

CHAPTER 4

Support

Ruth O'Donnell and
Lawrence Webster

M any sources of support are available to the library interested in adaptive equipment for people with disabilities. This chapter will discuss two types of support: informational support from organizations and corporations and funding support from public and private resources.

Since library professionals are often unfamiliar with the equipment and technology that can be used in a library to make collections, services, and programs accessible for people with disabilities, managers can benefit from time spent studying adaptive equipment options. Many disability interest groups exist that can be very helpful. *Self-advocacy groups* for persons with a particular type of disability usually have a national-level contact and can provide information on equipment that is favored by people who have that type of disability.

Organizations and corporations that provide services to people with disabilities and to their families and caregivers are also excellent resources for information. The *manufacturers and distributors of equipment* have a great deal of information, not only about their own products, but also, through their trade association publications, about all the products available of each equipment type. Beyond the organizations of and for people with disabilities and the vendors of auxiliary equipment, there are *national networks* established specifically for the purpose of providing information on existing and developing technology.

Library managers may be just as concerned about how to financially afford the adaptive equipment their library users need as about getting information about equipment. Funding comes from either internal sources—the public funds that support a state or locally provided library service, or external sources such as public or private grant funds and donations from philanthropic and community groups. Good public relations are the cornerstone of successful fund-raising to meet the need for providing adaptive equipment and services.

Organizations

Self-advocacy Groups

Americans who have disabilities and their families have banded together in special interest groups to support one another's needs and to advocate those needs to the rest of the public and to government agencies. Self-advocacy groups tend to focus on a particular type of disability. Self-Help for Hard of Hearing People is an example of a self-advocacy group. SHHH, as they call themselves, advocates for individuals who have hearing loss but are not deaf. Often the condition that causes the disability common to the members of a self-advocacy group is a part of the name of the group, such as the American Council of the Blind.

Groups whose members share a common disability generally have a broad array of interests. At the national level they work for legislation and funding for services needed by people who have that disability and for their rights to access services already available to non-disabled people. National organizations often put on an annual conference at which people who have the disability and service providers participate in programs and vendors demonstrate the latest in adaptive equipment. Self-advocacy groups also publish reviews of and articles about equipment and many have a periodic publication in which equipment vendors advertise and research or informational articles are published.

At the local level, self-advocacy groups are much more involved in individual needs and often serve a social as well as an advocacy purpose. They network with other self-advocacy groups, with community service agencies and clubs, and with the public and private schools. Members can provide a lot of information on local sources of adaptive equipment, places to get equipment repaired, and even their own experiences with particular products. Often the latter information is very valuable to library staff who have never even seen the equipment they are purchasing, much less used it enough to be able to assess the quality.

Service, Information, and Vendor Groups

Service groups for a particular type of disability or for people with any kind of disability are another type of organization that can be a resource for information on adaptive equipment. Sometimes service groups are also self-advocacy groups and take on some level of advocacy for the people they serve. Local Associations for Retarded Citizens (ARCs) are self-advocacy groups in that individuals and their parents or caregivers often make up the core of group membership, but the organizations also have a service role. They employ staff to operate residential and work programs for children and adults who are developmentally disabled.

Because organizations that provide services to individuals with disabilities are often working to meet information needs, they produce newsletters, hold group programs, maintain equipment and other product catalogs and samples, and generally do a lot of things that the library could help to support. The library can benefit from their work as well, by using service organization staff expertise during equipment selection and purchasing.

There is another type of organization that people with disabilities rely on for information and support. The Disability Rights Education and Defense Fund is an example of this kind of resource. While some of the people who work there have a disability and are, in a way, self-advocating, a main purpose of the organization is to provide information and training on the rights of persons who have disabilities.

Many other such agencies exist and some have national networks. They are often established as a nonprofit entity supported by contributions, federal grants, fees, self-advocacy group national headquarters, or affiliation with a research university. Some are branches of federal and state agencies. All are excellent sources of the latest information on technology for people with disabilities and the public and private programs that assist people and agencies to secure that technology.

How to Connect with Disability Interest Groups

To Contact Local or State Groups

Ask a library user or a personal acquaintance who has a disability if he or she belongs to or knows of any local groups or organizations.

Use the telephone book, the Chamber of Commerce, local outlets of state agencies, the school system, the health department, Goodwill, college and university service centers for students with disabilities, and other community information sources to locate your local or regional branch of a particular organization.

Call the state human services agency or agencies to get their lists.

To Contact National Groups

Some publications that identify and locate national disability groups:

Directory of National Organizations and Centers of and for Deaf and Hard of Hearing People. Washington, D.C.: Gallaudet University, National Information Center on Deafness.

Exceptional Parent. September issue each year publishes a Directory of National Organizations.

National Information and Advocacy Organizations. Washington, D.C.: Library of Congress, National Library Service for the Blind and Physically Handicapped, 1990

Wright, Kieth C. and Judith F. Davie. *Library Manager's Guide to Hiring and Serving Disabled Persons.* Jefferson, N.C.: McFarland, 1990.

Technology Information Centers and Networks

The last several years have seen a proliferation of resource centers, technology demonstration centers, and private industry disability centers. Federal grants have established networks of state level centers. All of these can be used by libraries looking for the most up-to-date information on technology and adaptive devices. The major government and privately supported centers are listed below.

Public Sector Resources

Alliance for Technology Access, 2173 E. Franciso Blvd., Suite L, San Rafael, CA 94901. (415) 455-4575. A project of the Foundation for Technology Access.

State level resource centers demonstrate adaptive equipment and technology, provide free information, and consult with consumers and others about access needs.

American Foundation for the Blind National Technology Center, 15 W. 16th St., New York, NY 10011. (212) 620-2080 or (800) 232-5463.

Free information on adaptive technology that assists people who are blind or have vision loss. Reviews of equipment by people who use it regularly.

Clearinghouse on Computer Accommodation, U.S. General Services Administration, 18th and F St., Room 1234, Washington, DC 20405. (202) 501-4906 (V/TDD). Susan A. Brummel, Director.

The clearinghouse works with all federal agencies to support implementation of the Federal Telecommunications System (FTS) 2000, to integrate voice, text, and video services throughout the government.

High-Tech Center for the Disabled. 21050 McClellan Rd., Cupertino, CA 95014. (408) 996-4636. Carl Brown, Director.

This center was established with a five year grant (through 1995) to provide a high tech training center where community college faculty come to learn how to employ high tech equipment and techniques to assist students with disabilities in California's community colleges. Faculty from around the state come to a variety of workshops and conferences here. Brown and others have published *Computer Access in Higher Education for Students with Disabilities.* The center also publishes a quarterly newsletter that is distributed statewide to all community college faculty.

National Information Center on Deafness, Gallaudet University, 800 Florida Ave. NE, Washington, DC 20002-3625. (202) 651-5051 (voice); (202) 651-5052 (TDD).

Inexpensive information on adaptive equipment for people who are deaf or hard of hearing.

National Rehabilitation Information Center, 8455 Colesville Rd., Suite 935, Silver Spring, MD 20910. (301) 588-9284 (voice or TDD); (301) 587-1967 (Fax).

A major resource referral center that maintains a clearinghouse on available equipment. Operates ABLEDATA, a computerized database on equipment and resources. ABLEDATA is accessible by modem or Internet. (See chapter 5, Electronic Resources)

National Technology Center, American Foundation for the Blind, 15 W. 16th St., New York, NY 10011. (212) 620-2080; (212) 620-2137 (Fax).

Supports three major divisions: Research and Development, Evaluations, and Information Systems. Evaluations are published in the *Journal of Visual Impairment and Blindness,* available in print, braille, or cassette. Also supports the Careers and Technology Information Bank (CTIB) that provides support for people needing to use adaptive equipment in various jobs or educational settings.

RESNA Technical Assistance Project, 1101 Connecticut Ave. NW, Suite 700, Washington, DC 20036. (202) 857-1140 (voice/TDD).

Thirty-one states are funded (as of June, 1992) under the Technology-Related Assistance for Individuals with Disabilities Act of 1988 to establish consumer-responsive statewide programs of technology-related assistance. The RESNA Technical Assistance Project has information about each state's efforts. Many state participants have technology demonstration capabilities.

Private Sector Resources

AT & T Accessible Communications Product Center, 5 Wood Hollow Rd., Room 1119, Parsippany, NJ 07054. (800) 233-1222 (voice); (800) 833-3232 (TDD).

Free information on telecommunications products for people who are deaf or hard of hearing.

Closing the Gap, P.O. Box 68, Henderson, MN 56044. (612) 248-3294; (612) 248-3810 (Fax).

Sponsors an annual conference with many exhibitors that features the latest adaptive equipment and technology. Usually held in October in Minneapolis.

Electronic Industries Association, Consumer Electronics Group, 2001 Pennsylvania Ave. NW, Washington, DC 20006-1813. (202) 457-4919.

Publishes inexpensive information on electronic equipment used by people with disabilities. Their brochure, "Extend Their Reach," sells for less than a dollar and is an excellent training tool.

Worldwide Disability Solutions Group at Apple Computer, Inc., 20525 Mariani Ave., Cupertino, CA 95014. (408) 974-7910.

Free information on software and hardware used with Apple and Macintosh computers.

Financial Support

Libraries seeking funds to acquire adaptive equipment for people with disabilities can turn to a wide variety of sources, public and private, at the local, state, and national levels.

Public Funds

Because of the force of law behind the Americans with Disabilities Act (ADA) and its attendant regulations, governmental and other public entities are highly motivated to provide at least such equipment as is necessary to meet minimum compliance guidelines.

The routine library planning and budgeting process is the first, most obvious source of funds for adaptive technology at this level. Libraries know what equipment and services they must provide to comply with the law, and both short- and long-range financial plans should reflect this knowledge.

Many libraries of all types are finding that cooperative efforts with other agencies in their parent institutions offer a cost-effective way of funding the acquisition of adaptive technologies. For example, if the library is an arm of city or county government or part of a larger institution such as a university, a total ADA compliance program for that government or university may simply include the library. Alternatively, the library might take a leadership role in the institution's ADA program by organizing and managing the adaptive technology efforts for the entire institution.

On the state and national levels, public libraries may look to Library Service and Construction Act funds under Title I, Public Library Services, and in some cases, Title II, Construction. These funds are generally administered through the state library agency.

The *Catalog of Federal Domestic Assistance* lists a host of federal grants programs, many of which are appropriate for acquisition of adaptive resources and retro-fitting of buildings to comply with ADA regulations. A significant example is the Community Development Block Grant Program, funded by the Department of Housing and Urban Development and administered by local government agencies. Many producers and vendors of adaptive equipment provide suggestions on funding sources as a part of their total marketing and promotion package.

Private Funds

Nonprofit organizations in the United States reap hundreds of billions of dollars every year from private sources—individuals, corporations, and foundations. Private funding can enable libraries of all types to broaden their resources and adaptive equipment for people with disabilities.

Locally, the Lions Clubs International have a long history of supporting low-vision adaptive devices. Many communities have community foundations, local family trusts, and service clubs. The medical community is a good source of funding for adaptive devices as well: doctors, optometrists, medical equipment purveyors, all like the positive public relations benefits of having their name associated with the library.

There are many opportunities for creative public-private collaboration in funding assistive technology. For example, a public library might develop a low-vision center in conjunction with a local Chamber of Commerce and its medical members; an academic library might look to a school of medicine, pharmacy, or physical therapy as a partner in establishing an "access center" for adaptive resources. Both the library and its partners benefit through positive public image, and the community benefits through enhanced adaptive resources.

National Resources

Nationally, the first place to look for information on private funding sources is the Foundation Center and its cooperating collections network. The center offers extensive, in-depth information on foundation and corporate philanthropy through four libraries (New York, San Francisco, Cleveland, and Washington), and more than 180 cooperative collections in all 50 states.

The center also publishes a host of basic and detailed works on funding sources, including the annual *Foundation Directory, A Nonprofit Organization Operating Manual: Planning for Survival and Growth, The Foundation Center's User-Friendly Guide: A Grantseeker's Guide to Resources*. Specialized guides include directories of funding sources in health, education, social services, religion, aging, arts and culture, and the *National Guide to Funding for Libraries and Information Services*. Publications are available in center libraries and cooperating collections. Center staff will provide research assistance. Two online databases are available through DIALOG: *The Foundation Directory and the Foundation Grants Index*.

The following resource list should help any library get started in raising the necessary funds for adaptive equipment and programs.

Organizations

Council on Foundations
1828 L St. NW
Washington, DC 20036
(202) 466-6512

Founded in 1949, the Council is a membership organization for grant-makers. An extensive list of publications includes works on management, corporate giving, community foundations, and other grant-making organizations.

The Foundation Center
79 Fifth Ave.
New York, NY 10003-3076
(800) 424-9836

Nonprofit organization providing information on private grant-making nationwide through a network of 185 cooperating libraries and nonprofit information centers.

The Grantsmanship Center
1125 W. 6th St., 5th Floor
P.O. Box 17220
Los Angeles, CA 90017
(213) 482-9860 (Voice)
(213) 482-9863 (Fax)

Provides publications, workshops, and technical assistance in proposal development, successful program design.

Independent Sector
1828 L St. NW, No. 1200
Washington, DC 20036
(202) 223-8100

Membership organization of foundations, corporate giving programs, and voluntary organizations. Extensive publications list includes *Giving and Volunteering in the United States, The Nonprofit Almanac 1992–1993; Dimensions of the Independent Sector; The Board Member's Book* by Brian O'Connell; and *The Nonprofit Lobbying Guide.*

National Center for Nonprofit Boards
2000 L St. NW, Suite 510
Washington, DC 20036
(202) 452-6262

Provides technical assistance and support to nonprofit boards of all types in governance, structure, fund-raising, and related topics.

National Charities Information Bureau, Inc.
19 Union Square West
New York, NY 10003-3395
(212) 929-6300 (Voice)
(212) 463-7083 (Fax)

Founded in 1918 to provide prospective donors information on the soundness of individual nonprofit groups. THE NCIB evaluates charities on the basis of such criteria as governance, fiscal responsibility, and mission.

National Organization on Disability
910 16th St., NW, Suite 600
Washington, DC 20006
(202) 293-5960
(202) 293-5968 (TDD)
(202) 293-7999 (Fax)

The National Organization on Disability supports communities' efforts to provide services and technology for persons with a wide variety of disabilities. Annual competition for cash awards is divided among communities greater and less than 50,000 population. Grant prize annually is $10,000. A quarterly newsletter, *NOD Report,* provides information about the competition.

The Society for Nonprofit Organizations
6314 Odana Rd., Suite 1
Madison, WI 53719
(608) 274-9777

A service organization founded in 1983 with the purpose of promoting excellence in leadership, management, and governance. Publishes a monthly journal, *Nonprofit World,* and provides individual technical assistance to member organizations.

U.S. General Services Administration
Federal Domestic Assistance Catalog Staff
Ground Floor, Reporters Bldg.
300 7th St. SW
Washington, DC 20407
(800) 669-8831

Publishes the annual compendium of federal grant programs. Also provides online tailored information through the *Federal Assistance Programs Retrieval System.*

Publications

Chronicle of Philanthropy
P.O. Box 1989
Marion, Ohio 43306-4089
Biweekly

Corporate Philanthropy Report
2727 Fairview Ave. East
Seattle, WA 98102
Monthly except September and
    January

Journal of Volunteer Administration
Association for Volunteer
Administration
P.O. Box 4584
Boulder, CO 80306
(303) 541-0238

*Nonprofit World: The National Nonprofit
    Leadership and Management Journal*
The Society for Nonprofit
Organizations
6314 Odana Rd., Suite 1
Madison, WI 53719
(608) 274-9777

Philanthropy Monthly
P.O. Box 989
New Milford, CT 06776
Ten issues per year

DIRECTORIES, HANDBOOKS, AND GUIDES

Catalog of Federal Domestic Assistance. Annual. Washington, D.C.: United States Government Printing Office.

The Foundation Directory and *The Foundation Directory Supplement.* New York: The Foundation Center, 1992.

Howe, Fisher. *The Board Member's Guide to Fund Raising: What Every Trustee Needs to Know about Raising Money.* San Francisco: Jossey-Bass, 1991.

The National Guide to Funding for Elementary and Secondary Education. New York: The Foundation Center, 1991.

The National Guide to Funding for Libraries and Information Services. New York: The Foundation Center, 1991.

The National Guide to Funding in Aging, 2nd ed. New York: The Foundation Center, 1992.

The National Guide to Funding in Health, 2nd ed. New York: The Foundation Center, 1990.

The National Guide to Funding in Higher Education, 2nd ed. New York: The Foundation Center, 1992.

Nonprofit Almanac, 1992–1993: Dimensions of the Independent Sector, ed. Virginia Ann Hodgkinson, et al. San Francisco: Jossey Bass, 1992.

Payton, Robert L. *Philanthropy: Voluntary Action for the Public Good.* New York: American Council on Education/Macmillan, 1988.

Shannon, James P., ed. *The Corporate Contributions Handbook: Devoting Private Means to Public Needs.* San Francisco: Jossey-Bass, 1991.

CHAPTER 5

Adaptive Technology Resources

Dennis A. Norlin

T his chapter provides a highly selective list of resources designed to provide a basic collection of information on adaptive equipment and technology for all libraries. It is divided into five major categories:

Monographs

Nonprint Resources

Electronic Resources

Newsletters/Journals

Government Agencies

All of these resources are carefully targeted to the topic of adaptive equipment and technology for libraries to use in providing services for librarians and employees with disabilities. Materials that discuss disabilities outside of the library setting, or that focus primarily on aspects of disabilities other than adaptive equipment and technology are purposely omitted. Libraries should be able to obtain these materials readily and at little or no cost; they represent the authors' recommendations of what are the essential resources in this field.

Monographs

Americans with Disabilities Act Handbook. Equal Employment Opportunity Commission and the U. S. Department of Justice. EEOC-BK-19. Washington, D.C.: U. S. Government Printing Office, 1991.

> The *ADA Handbook* is the single most valuable resource libraries can acquire to prepare themselves to respond to the letter and the spirit of the Americans with Disabilities Act. Not only does the handbook provide an excellent historical overview of the ADA's development, it also includes full text of the accompanying regulations on accessibility and architectural barriers, diagrams of accessibility requirements, and a summary of regulations and their effective dates.

Assistive Technology: A Selective Bibliography. Washington, D.C.: Library of Congress, National Library Services for the Blind and Physically Handicapped, 1992. No. 92–1.

> The most current bibliography available from the Library of Congress, this 18-page bibliography covers the period 1985–1990, and contains brief abstracts for each article, book, or pamphlet it lists, arranged alphabetically by author. It also contains a useful list of 13 magazines on assistive devices and products, 16 "Sources for Further Information," and a list of other Library of Congress publications in the areas of disabilities.

Baskin, Barbara H. and Karen H. Harris, eds. *The Mainstreamed Library: Issues, Ideas, Innovations.* Chicago: American Library Association, 1982.

> This book is dated, certainly, yet it is still an important addition to any collection on adaptive equipment and technology. Analysis of the physical environment, materials selection criteria, programs, and outreach are all of permanent value, and the sections on technology and software introduce the use of both high tech and low tech ideas that can be used especially with children.

Black, J. B., Janet Black, Ruth O'Donnell, and Jane Scheuerle. *Surveying Public Libraries for the ADA.* Tallahassee, Florida: Bureau of Library Development, Division of Library and Information Services, 1992.

> This document was designed to help Florida public libraries develop a reasonable and thoughtful response to the ADA by developing a self-evaluation survey, a plan of service, and provisions for staff training and public relations. It includes a brief chapter on "Auxiliary Aids and Services," and an excellent, current bibliography.

Brown, et al. *Computer Access in Higher Education for Students with Disabilities: A Practical Guide to the Selection and Use of Adapted Computer Technology,* 2nd ed. Monterey, Calif.: California Community College, Chancellor's Office, 1987.

Brown, director of the High-Tech Center for the Disabled (California Community Colleges Chancellor's Office, Cupertino), and a number of colleagues provide information about input devices, keyboards, software options, and legal and logistical requirements for academic computing for persons with visual, mild-to-moderate and moderate-to-severe orthopedic, learning, and other disabilities.

Directory of National Sources on Disabilities, 5th ed. Washington, D.C.: Conwal Incorporated for the National Institute on Disability and Rehabilitation Research of the Office of Special Education and Rehabilitative Services of the Department of Education, 1991.

A standard reference work with the intent of providing exhaustive coverage of national programs, this directory attempts to identify and describe all organizations supplying disability-related information, referral, and direct human services. Organized according to the pattern of the *Dictionary of Occupational Titles.* A number of indexes provide a variety of access points to information.

Foos, Donald D. and Nancy C. Pack, eds. *How Libraries Must Comply with the Americans with Disabilities Act* (ADA). Phoenix: Oryx Press, 1992.

The authors have sought to provide libraries with a clear and effective guide to the Americans with Disabilities Act of 1990. Michael Gunde's opening chapter outlining the act and Ruth O'Donnell's guidelines for planning and implementing the act are the most usable; Peter Manheimer's chapter on legal implications is the most scholarly and readable.

Lazzaro, Joseph J. *Adaptive Technologies for Learning and Work Environments.* Chicago: American Library Association, 1993.

An excellent overview of the history of adaptive technology and a discussion of the contexts in which specific technologies are helpful and useful.

Library Hi Tech. Special issue: Volume 11, no. 1, 1993.

Entire issue devoted to issues of computing, technology, and disabilities.

Lovejoy, Eunice G. *Portraits of Library Service to People with Disabilities.* Boston: G. K. Hall, 1990.

This book contains descriptions of several "success stories" in library services for persons with disabilities, affording librarians the opportunity to examine a variety of program options, from special needs centers to mainstreamed services. As background material and as an inspiration to other libraries to provide such services, Lovejoy's readable volume is a good place to begin.

Managing Information Resources for Accessibility. Washington, D.C.: Clearinghouse on Computer Accommodation (COCA), Information Resources Management Service (IRMS), U.S. General Services Administration (GSA), 1991.

This handbook provides guidance to federal managers unfamiliar with the policy and practice of information accessibility to accommodate users with disabilities and to provide for their effective access to information resources. Available from GSA: Susan A. Brummel, Director, Clearinghouse on Computer Accommodation, Room 2022, KGDO, 18th and F Streets NW, Washington, DC 20405. (202) 501-4905; (202) 501-2010 (TDD).

Mates, Barbara T. *Library Technology for Visually and Physically Impaired Patrons.* Westport and London: Meckler, 1991.

A concise, well-illustrated guide to the explosion in new assistive technology and equipment, Mates's book will serve as an excellent introduction for libraries wanting to know "what's out there?" Based on her convictions that the fastest growing group needing library and print access is the visually impaired (p. 8) and that the most critical gap in the National Library Service for the Blind and Physically Handicapped Network's service has been its inability to provide timely and quick reference service to its patrons (p. ix), Mates devotes a great deal of attention to computer hardware and software and CD-ROM products, since "the advancements (with adaptions) are enabling the disabled population to access and assimilate virtually any title on disc (either CD-ROM disc or PC diskette)."

Mates describes (and often illustrates) both the generic types of technology available and a number of specific products currently produced, often with evaluative comments based upon testing by centers like the National Technology Center of the American Foundation for the Blind. The primary focus of the book is on visual impairments with separate chapters on Large Print Access, Braille Access, Optical Character Recognition Systems, Keyboards, and Processing Information without a Keyboard. Appendices include a list of Vendors and Distributors, CD-ROM Titles That Translate into a Special Format, Bulletin Boards, and Funding Sources for Adaptive Equipment.

McNulty, Tom and Dawn M. Suvino. *Access to Information: Materials, Technologies, and Services for Print-Impaired Readers.* Chicago: American Library Association, Library and Information Technology Association, 1993.

A guide to "materials, technologies, and services for print-impaired readers." Provides an introduction to computer literacy, and separate chapters on tactile, audio, and low vision materials and methods.

Walling, Linda Lucas. *Disabilities, Children, and Libraries: Mainstreaming Services in Public Libraries and School Library Media Centers.* Englewood, Colo.: Libraries Unlimited, Inc. 1993.

This welcome new revision of Lucas and Karrenbrock's 1983 book, *The Disabled Child in the Library: Moving into the Mainstream,* is a basic primer on library services for children with disabilities. It provides at least brief identification of a wide variety of disabilities that librarians are likely to encounter, and includes a helpful section on toys, games, and puzzles for children with disabilities.

Nonprint Resources

And Access for All: ADA and Your Library. Color. 45 min. American Library Association/Library Video Network. 320 York Rd., Towson, MD 21204. 800-441-TAPE. 163p. resource guide. $130

"It's not right because it's the law; it's the law because it's right:" that's this film's compelling conclusion. A fitting sequel to *People First, and Access for All* provides both the incentive and a plan for libraries to implement both the letter and the spirit of ADA.

Children with Special Needs. PBS VIDEO. Available from PBS VIDEO, 1320 Braddock Place, Alexandria, VA 22314-1698. (800) 424-7963.

This new catalog includes a wide variety of film titles on disabilities, racism, and justice issues.

People First: Serving and Employing People with Disabilities. ALA Video. Chicago: American Library Association, 1990. ISBN 8389-2113-2.

This 38-minute film, produced in Maryland, is an excellent introduction to the attitudinal barriers that prevent full service to and employment of people with disabilities in libraries. Excellent for in-service education or for initiating a program of response to the needs of persons with disabilities.

Special Feelings. Philadelphia: Temple University Department of Radio-Television Film, 1987. Dirk Eitzen, producer. Available from Indiana University Audio-Visual Center, Bloomington, Ind.

A moving 28-minute film that shows and discusses the emotions and relationships of persons with a variety of disabilities. Although the film focuses primarily on relationships between people with disabilities, it shows them in a wide variety of settings utilizing many different types of adaptive equipment and technology.

Workplace of the '90s. Mountain View, Calif.: Telesensory, 1992. (800) 227-8418.

Ten-minute video demonstrating a variety of adaptive computing equipment used by visually impaired employees at several different companies. Excellent demonstration of everything from closed circuit television (CCT) with magnification to computers that produce braille or synthetic speech.

Electronic Resources

Christopher Lewis

Joining Listservs

Listservs are programs that act as message switches for e-mail messages for e-mail on specific subjects. To subscribe to a listserv, send an e-mail message to the listserv using the message SUBSCRIBE [NAME OF LISTSERV]

To subscribe to **adapt-l**, for example, you would use the telnet facility of e-mail:

mail adapt-l@auvm.american.edu

You can leave the SUBJECT line blank.

At the blank line type subscribe adapt-l

You then type a single period [.], ENTER,

a second period [.], and you'll be added to the listserv of your choice.

WIDNET

An expanded list of listservs is published by the Disability Policy Network, a service of the World Institute on Disability (WID); 510 16th St., Oakland, CA 94612-1500.

To receive a copy of WIDLIST via Internet send mail to widnet@delphi.com and type "Request WIDLIST" as the subject or body of your message.

adapt-l@auvm   [bitnet]
adapt-l@auvm.american.edu   [internet]
> LITA Adaptive Technologies Interest Group. Discussion about adaptive technologies, both low and high tech.

ada-law@ndsuvmi   [bitnet]
ada-law@vm1.NoDak.edu   [internet]
> Discussion group about any aspect of ADA and any other disability-related legislation

axslib-L@sjuvm.stjohns.edu   [internet]
axslib-l@sjuvm   [bitnet]
> Project EASI: Library Access for Persons with Disabilities. A very active list-server focusing on topics related to improving computer accessibility for college/university faculty and students.

backs-l@uvmvm   [bitnet]
backs-l@moose.uvm.edu   [internet]
> Research on low back pain and related disabilities

blindws@ndsuvm1   [bitnet]
blindnws@vm1.nodak.edu   [internet]
> Blind News Digest

blind-l@uafsysb.uark.edu   [internet]

bliss-l@brownvm   [bitnet]
bliss-l@brownvm.brown.edu   [internet]
> Barus Lab Interactive Speech System List

braintmr@mitvma.mit.edu   [internet]
> Devoted to brain tumor research and support

cfs-news@nihlist   [bitnet]
cfs-news@list.nih.gov   [internet]
> Chronic Fatigue Syndrome Newsletter

cfs-l@nihlist   [bitnet]
cfs-l@list.nih.gov   [internet]
   Chronic Fatigue Syndrome Discussion Group

ddfind-l@gitvm1   [bitnet]
   Information Networking on Disabilities

deaf-l@siucvmb   [bitnet]
deaf-l@siucvmb.siu.edu   [internet]
   Deaf List

deafblnd@ukcc.uky.edu   [internet]
   A list for individuals who are both deaf and blind

easi@sjuvm.stjohns.edu   [internet]
easi@sjuvm   [bitnet]
   EASI (Equal Access to Software and Information) is a production of EDUCOM,
   and contains discussion among educators about a wide variety of disabilities.

L-hcap@ndsuvm1   [bitnet]
L-hcap@vm1.nodak.edu   [internet]
   Handicap Digest. General discussion of many topics related to individuals with
   disabilities in education.

libref-f@kentvm   [bitnet]
   Discussion of library reference issues

scr-l@mizzoui   [bitnet]
   Study of cognitive rehabilitation

slling-l@yalevm   [bitnet]
   Sign language linguistics list

sorehand@ucsfvm   [bitnet]
   Discussion of carpal tunnel syndrome, tendinitis, etc.

stroke-l@ukcc   [bitnet]
   Stroke discussion list

Bulletin Boards

ABLE INFORM contains: ABLEDATA—a database of 18,000 assistive device descriptions; REHABDATA—a literature database of 40,000 abstracts of reports, articles, and books; NARIC GUIDE TO PERIODICALS—a database of serial publication titles; NIDRR DIRECTORY—a collection of information about the projects funded by the National Institute on Disability and Rehabilitation Research; and NARIC KNOWLEDGEBASE—an information and referral database in disability/rehabilitation. Modem access: (301) 589-3563 (N-8-1). Also accessible through telnet: **fedworld.gov**; from TOP menu choose DD 115. For assistance with Abledata telnet: **naric@cap.gwu.edu**.

THE HANDICAP NEWS. Modem access: (300 – 1440 baud, 24 hours) (203) 926-6168.

Gopher

Cornucopia of Disability Information (CODI)

CODI is a gopher that provides a wide variety of disability-related information to local (SUNY Buffalo), state, region, and national patrons. The main menu has 22 items ranging from the National Information Sources on Disabilities publication of NIDRR to a national TDD telephone directory. To reach CODI from another gopher system type **gopher val-dor.cc.buffalo.edu 70**. From a non-gopher site type **telnet panda.uiowa.edu**. Then follow the menu directions: 4 = Online Info/9 = Other Gopher Servers/2 = North America/3 = USA/1 = All/then cursor to Cornucopia.

Deaf Gopher

A gopher service for the deaf and persons with hearing impairment. Although much of the information is local (Michigan) Deaf Gopher also has a growing number of national resources.

Telnet to **gopher.msu.edu** (Michigan State University). Login as **gopher**. Follow three menus in order: *Information for the MSU Community/ MSU College & Departmental Information/DEAF GOPHER*.

EASI

A gopher service provided through St. John's University in New York, EASI contains a menu system of information sources that includes "Library Publications and Access Issues." EASI also lists conferences and workshops in adaptive technology. It is an excellent, current source for information on disabilities. From a gopher server, choose New York State and then locate St. John's University's gopher and follow the directions to the EASI gopher.

FTP

handicap.shel.isc-br.com
IP address: 129.189.4.184

Files on this machine duplicate Handicap News BBS. Includes the complete text of ADA, screen readers, speech synthesizer drivers, IBM Disability Resource Center guides, various newsletters; more than 800 files. For information contact Bill McGarry (203) 337-1518, **wtm@bunker.shel.isc-br.com**

handicap.afd.olivetti.com

Log in as **anonymous**; use your e-mail address as password. Mast index lists all 800 files and programs in the file "/PUB/INDEX." There are more than 60 directories. Each has an index file that is called "00-INDEX.TXT."

Newsletters/Journals

Assistive Technology Journal. Quarterly publication of Rehabilitation Engineering Society of North America (RESNA), 1101 Connecticut Ave. NW, Suite 700, Washington, DC 20036 (202) 857-1199.

Closing the Gap. Bimonthly publication of Closing the Gap, P.O. Box 68, Henderson, MN 56044. (612) 248-3294; (612) 248-3810 (Fax). Magazine focuses on computer hardware and software for persons with all types of disabilities. Sponsors an annual conference, also called CLOSING THE GAP each October in Minneapolis that features the latest adaptive equipment from many vendors. Subscription cost: $26.

Information Technology and Disabilities. A new refereed journal devoted to the practical and theoretical issues surrounding the development and effective use of new and emerging technologies by computer users with disabilities. Founded by EASI (Equal Access to Software and Information). Tom McNulty, editor-in-chief, Bopst Library, New York University, 70 Washington Square South, New York, NY 10012. (212) 998-2519 (voice); (212) 998-4980 (TDD). Internet: Mcnulty@acfcluster.nyu.edu. Bitnet: Mcnulty@Nyuacf

Journal of the Association for Persons with Severe Handicaps. Quarterly publication of the Association for Persons with Severe Handicaps (TASH), 7010 Roosevelt Way NE, Seattle, WA 98115. (202) 523-8446.

Library Access: Services for People with Disabilities. Institute for the Study of Developmental Disabilities, 2853 E. 10th St., Bloomington, IN 47405. (812) 855-6508. Marilyn Irwin, editor. The quarterly eight-page newsletter of the library at the Institute for the Study of Developmental Disabilities, this publication often includes information about laws affecting libraries and people with disabilities, lists of resources for a wide variety of disabilities, and descriptions of grants and projects involving librarians and developmental disabilities.

OSERS News in Print. Newsletter of the Clearinghouse on Disability Information, U.S. Department of Education, Office of Special Education and Rehabilitative Services, Switzer Bldg., Room 3132, Washington, DC 20202-2524. (202) 732-1241.

Rehabilitation Newsletter. Bimonthly publication of the National Institute for Rehabilitation Engineering, P.O. Box T, Hewitt, NJ 07421. (201) 853-6585.

TASH Newsletter. Publication of the Association for Persons with Severe Handicaps (TASH), 7010 Roosevelt Way NE, Seattle, WA 98115. (202) 523-8446.

Very Special Arts. Triannual publication of Very Special Arts, John F. Kennedy Center for the Performing Arts, Education Office, Washington, DC 20566. (202) 628-2800.

Government Agencies

Department of Education

Rehabilitation Services Administration
    Acting Commissioner Howard Moses
    3028 Mary E. Switzer Bldg.
    330 C St., SW
    Washington, DC 20202
    (202) 205-5482

National Institute on Disability and Rehabilitation Research
Director Kathryn D. Seelman
3060 Mary E. Switzer Bldg.
330 C St., S.W.
Washington, DC 20202
(202) 205-8134

Department of Health and Human Services

Administration for Developmental Disabilities
Commissioner Bob Williams
3150 Hubert H. Humphrey Bldg.
200 Independence Ave. SW
Washington, DC 20201
(202) 690-6590

Department of Labor

The President's Committee on Employment of People with Disabilities
Chairman Tony Coelho
300 1331 F St. NW
Washington, DC 20004-1107
(800) 232-9675 (Voice or TDD)
(202) 376-6200
(202) 376-6205 (TDD)
(202) 376-6219 (Fax)

National Council on Disability

Acting Executive Director Edward Burke
1331 F St. N.W.
Suite 1050
Washington, DC 20004
(202) 272 2004

Office of Technology Assessment

Director Roger C. Herdman
5th Floor
600 Pennsylvania Ave. SE
Washington, DC 20003
(202) 224-3695

INDEX A

Vendors That Specialize in Technology for Specific Disabilities

Numbers refer to Vendor Identification
Number in Chapter 3

Specific Product Names

Numbers refer to Vendor Identification
Number in Chapter 3

Type of Equipment or Technology

Numbers refer to Vendor Identification
Number in Chapter 3